By Onny, Teme
and Clun

~

BY ONNY, TEME AND CLUN

≈ Flyfishing in the valley of the Teme ≈

by

G. R. LANE

With illustrations by the Author

For

K. D. Y.

~*~

All rights reserved. No part of this publication may be reproduced, stored in a retrieval system, or transmitted in any form or by any means, electronic, mechanical, photocopying, recording or otherwise, without the prior permission of the author.

Copyright © 2022 G R Lane

ISBN: 978 1 7391353 0 0

Cover photograph by Alex

CONTENTS

	Page
Preamble	1
An Introduction	8

PART I

Spring	12
An Opening Day on the Rea	20
A Fish for Good Friday	32
Summer	43
By Onny	48
By Onny with a Fly	52
The River Corve	65
The Clun River	73
An Evening Rise on the Rea	94
An Evening on the Teme	108
Autumn	126
Grayling below the Aqueduct	131
Winter	157
Closed-season	159

PART II

On Rods	167
On Reels	181
On Lines, Leaders, and Tippets	185
On Knots and Tangles	194
Border Flies	204
On Dress	240
On Accessories	246

PART III

Tactics of the Minor Stream	258
A Final Cast	282

PREAMBLE

If one of the charms of angling is to seek beautiful fish in beautiful surroundings, then the quest for wild trout and grayling in the rivers and streams of the Teme valley is angling at its best.

This book is about angling on the waters of the Welsh borderlands, particularly the River Teme and its tributaries. The Teme, Onny, Clun, Rea and Corve are all included. At least one day on each is described to illustrate tactics and flies. Methods and tackle described have also met with success on similar waters in Devon, Derbyshire, Yorkshire and beyond.

Anyone starting angling will find the intimate nature of these border streams an ideal classroom. Catching a trout, or any fish, is not easy; however, trout in these border waters are plentiful and fishing pressure is light. The Teme is famous for its grayling, they complement the trout and extend the season into autumn, they can also be found in these pages. Few, if any, parts of the country have so many trout streams available and in such close proximity. The novice will find watercraft and knowledge of trout behaviour easier to learn here than on the windswept banks of a reservoir. They will learn in peace without a line of fishermen watching, or a costly day ticket every time they fish.

These border streams are special and require a particular approach. There are many books on fishing reservoirs and still-waters, but they will be little or no use when seeking instruction on a small stream. Chalk-streams too are very different from our border rivers, methods will have to be adapted and new skills learnt to be successful on rougher overgrown border rivers.

Few still-water flies will be suitable for border rivers. Typical chalk-stream flies may be used. Fly-dressers should modify the style of dressing to suit the water, that difference can turn a frustrating blank into a good day. The reader will find suitable patterns, including local unpublished fly patterns, explained along with descriptions of styles and tactics.

Too few books are written about these border streams despite the fact they are numerous, inexpensive and within reach of many. Perhaps there is a thought that all rivers, chalk-stream or rain fed, are the same: this will not do. The steady unbroken water of the chalk-stream, where individual fish can be spotted in deep water, is nothing like the tumbling border stream. Methods of fishing each are totally different. Chalk-streams are usually heavily fished, an angler on each beat every day, whereas some sections of the Teme and many smaller border streams are never fished at all, and many a trout never sees an angler's fly. The correct approach, adapting to the different challenges these small overgrown waters present, can bring excellent results: using the tackle and tactics of still-water or chalk-stream will lead to frustration and failure. A few good books have been written about border waters. Unfortunately, most of them are now dated, tactics and especially tackle has moved on.

Throughout I have often been aware that when it comes to advice, some are most keen to give what they most need themselves. So, these days by the river contain personal preferences, solutions suited to that particular day. If they can be repeated, that is all to the good. It is pointless to dictate what to do in each and every situation, even if that were possible. Any hints and tips offered come with appropriate deference that fellow anglers may know a way that works better for them. No one should think there is only one correct way of fishing or that they should not use an alternative that they enjoy more.

The recollection of days by the river may amuse some anglers and assist others; more detailed information can be found in the sections on tackle, tactics, flies, and the rest.

Tackle is described and consideration given to its suitability for border streams. It is not only frustrating to arrive at an unknown stream to find it heavily overgrown and to have brought along a rod too long to manage a cast, it is a waste of valuable time and money. Wading is detailed on various waters, the need for chestwaders, thighwaders or no waders at all, to avoid the annoyance of not being able to access all the water; also the safety of wading, to save a dip. The emphasis is low-cost, simple solutions for tackle and preparing the angler so they enjoy their time on the water.

Some of the ideas expressed herein may differ from accepted practice, indeed I hope they do, otherwise it all seems a waste of time. They differ simply because these waters are different from the standard river as described in most books.

When it came to choosing tactics, conventional or from experience, they were drawn from practical, personal experience every time. This local knowledge will assist the angler and they will, I hope, adapt the ideas to their own preferences.

Anglers with some experience of fly-fishing who want to move to fishing for wild trout will enjoy the choice of water. Rather than spacing themselves around a still-water they will be able to choose from miles of river bank where meeting another angler is a rare chance for a welcome chat.

Newcomers will see that the cost of fishing is a fraction of that of stocked still-waters or chalk-streams. One day on a famous chalk-stream beat can cost more than a whole year fishing on some border rivers and streams. Indeed there are many

many miles of free fishing on the Teme and other local streams. Sometimes fishing is available by simply asking the farmer, whilst many miles of good water are open to all for a few pounds.

You will not be led to all the best places, but you will have a glimpse so anyone who is keen can find them for themselves, and even better find their own best places. There are enough brooks, streams and rivers running through these Welsh marches to admit another true angler and enough trout swimming in them to last a lifetime's angling.

There is a growing appreciation of wild trout and the waters which contain them, but there is still a lack of understanding of the fishing border waters offer. The aim is to shine the spotlight on these rivers and streams and their splendid fishing. Although every angler has difficult days, the novice more than most, this advice and assistance should give hope that these waters are not impossible.

Come, walk these banks with me, you are welcome to look over my shoulder, share a rod

Preamble

and a few days on the water, for you are the ideal fishing companion, silent and invisible. Every day described has come from the fishing diary. This is a small book of small rivers, but frequently it is the small things that are important. So throw another log on the fire and enjoy.

AN INTRODUCTION

The aim of this book is to highlight the opportunities for anglers in the border region. However the reader may be curious as to my credentials to undertake this task.

As a boy I was fascinated by streams, paddling, building dams, and splashing stones; later after the present of a rod I came to fish. My first fish on rod and line was a minnow, caught on the River Teme below the castle, on a stretch of water called the Bread Walk. That was in late sixties, now fifty years later I still fish the Teme, and still catch minnows.

These border waters were for me an ideal introduction to a lifetime's angling pleasure. Although over many years I have been fortunate to visit many waters, from famous chalk-streams to moorland brooks, for me none can eclipse these South Shropshire streams. I have fished some of the very best chalk-streams due to the kindness and generosity of those running the fisheries. In return several very good chalk-stream anglers have fished

An Introduction

as my guest on these border streams and truly enjoyed their day. The rivers of the Teme valley are not inferior in providing pleasure, they are simply different. I enjoyed fishing the Test and Itchen, walking in the footsteps of Halford and Skues, but, if forced to choose one above the rest, it would be the little River Rea.

So here are some tales from the riverbank, days taken from the diary, along with a few hints and tips for a good day. I profess no great expertise with the rod (or pen) and the reader can expect to do just as well, if not better, than me. Any advantage I may have is down to experience; that experience and local knowledge I wish to share.

Through angling we meet many people and to all my friends who have offered support and advice, I thank you. This book couldn't have been written without you.

As to the writing, I have tried to hold back from using 'I'. It is irritating to be constantly reminded how 'I' landed this huge fish, 'I' invented this fly, or 'I' solved this problem or that. In the best fishing accounts it has been me, the reader who has been on the river bank, my red tipped float that dipped by the water lilies, my rod tip that flickered and was pulled around by chub or barbel, and my fly that floated over the trout.

This book was at first conceived as a short guide that might be of use to anglers joining the Tenbury Fishing Association; consequently many of the days described take place on Association waters.

The book also serves to call attention to the availability and promote the angling opportunities on the Teme and other local waters.

The Teme, like all rivers, needs anglers to support and defend it: all rivers are at risk without advocates.

The Tenbury Fishing Association, one of the oldest fishing associations in the country, is in constant need of new members.

Too often anglers are unaware of the potential of the river. Anglers had complained of lack of local advice and lacked the local knowledge to turn frustration into enjoyment.

These accounts are an attempt to show that good fishing in beautiful surroundings is available to all at low cost. It tells how, with a little effort

An Introduction

and endeavour, the waters of this area offer excellent rewards.

Local knowledge, descriptions of rivers, and suggestions of tackle, will guide the angler and save time and frustration. The experienced angler will know how valuable such knowledge can be, whilst the novice or complete beginner should be motivated to give these waters a trial. It is, in short, a book that would have been useful to me when starting out.

Finally, it is a record of my heartfelt appreciation for many happy days spread over fifty years of angling by Onny, Teme and Clun; a small tribute to this land 'of springs and rivers'.

It will not guarantee a fish every time, although there are fish in plenty, nor reveal the secret of catching monsters. Large fish come to me infrequently; memorable fish, all the time.

The true angler goes to the river to amuse himself, not to amaze others. This is a book less about fishing, more about angling. Many fish have been caught over the years; the fish were released to swim free: it is the angler who is still hooked.

SPRING

Spring, springtime, the very sound of it is exciting. After a long and wearing wait through the dark winter days, at last the season is about to start. Warmth is what every living thing has been waiting for. As the sun climbs a little higher in the sky and shines a little longer, we can look forward to the trout becoming active. The activity that best shows that trout are about and feeding, is a rise.

Being keen to fish as early as possible, it makes sense to head for the open riffles and glides where the sun warms the stones. Here the first insects crawl from their hides and feeding trout hover in the ripples.

The stream is much more open in spring with little bank growth and even the trees are without their canopy of leaves. In deep pools and where high banks or buildings cast shadows, the water is colder and little stirs.

The season starts a couple of weeks earlier over the hills, on the streams flowing into the Wye. On the first warm spring day it can be irresistible to

Spring

nip over to the Lugg or the Arrow for a few hours spring trout fishing. Here you will be fishing while the season for grayling is still open. Maybe it is the best of both worlds being able to fish for trout and still be happy with the occasional grayling.

Spring fishing is very weather dependant. Trout need some warmth to encourage them to move. However, the border trout are rarely out of condition early in the season. Maybe our small wild trout do not need the same amount of food as their southern counterparts to gain fitness. It could be there are more non-spawning fish amongst the small-stream trout. While the chalk-stream angler may wait until April or even May to cast a line, in the Teme valley March finds the angler at the waterside.

Like all ectothermic animals (with blood at ambient temperature), they are sluggish in the cold, and need a little heat. The magic number seems to be about fifty degrees Fahrenheit or the equivalent, ten degrees Celsius. No doubt you should measure the water temperature to find the correct level in the trout's own environment. Then, if you take the trouble to go to the river to take the temperature, you might as well fish. Therefore, rely on the weather forecast the night before, the thermometer in the porch, and how much you want to go fishing. Another variable in spring fishing is river levels. Water can be a good winter level or 'winter heavy', that is plenty of water but running clear, through to running 'red as a fox'. Coloured water kills the fishing. When the fields are waterlogged, a heavy shower in the morning can colour the streams in the afternoon and the rivers the next day. The water clears from the headwaters and the smaller streams first. The Lugg and Arrow often run clear when the Teme and its streams are coloured. They run through gravels rather than the Teme's clay soils. Conversely, the upper Teme around Knighton clears quickly, due again to it running over gravel.

Those days, when the early spring sun shines and encourages the nymphs to climb out from under stones to sunbathe and ripen ready for hatching, also stir the angler. Quite often the flies are up before the trout in the spring. In February and March there is often a brief hatch with no fish

Spring

rising. A hatch will appear most days in early spring between noon and two o'clock.

Teme trout are reluctant to rise at any time, and spring fishing is usually wet-fly or nymph. As to the species of fly hatching. If it is floating down the river in early spring, and it is not a duck, then it's a spring olive. Sometimes called a large dark olive, but as they are neither particularly large, nor dark, nor olive, then spring olive is the better name, and one that was used previously.

Spring olives on the Rea and other small streams are around hook size sixteen, or dressed 'small', on a size fourteen.

Other flies of the spring are the iron blue,[1] and the march brown. The iron blue used to hatch on the Rea but it is now rare in the Teme valley. It is a smaller fly, fitting a size eighteen hook. They are sold, dressed on a size fourteen, by retailers who have not actually seen an iron blue. Incidentally, an iron blue is not blue, neither is it iron. They are identifiable by their small size and their inky dark grey wings.

---

[1] Initials of natural flies are in lower case, artificial patterns in upper case.

The natural march brown is elusive. It is a fly of the larger rivers, rare on the Teme. It is more likely on the Wye or Usk than the smaller streams. It likes rocky, gravely reaches. They tend to appear in April rather than March, (but they are brown). So an artificial March Brown is probably a fly that is in most anglers fly boxes without being used to imitate the natural. That is not to say that the March Brown is not a good fly, in its smaller sizes it is probably taken for a spring olive. A simplified dressing that works well is the March Hare, an imitation of early olive nymphs.

A Silver March Brown can be a very good fly for trout and grayling. A very experienced angler who fished the Teme for many years reckoned that the three wet flies to have on your cast were a Silver March Brown on the 'bob', a Silver March Brown on the dropper and a Silver March Brown on the point.

Another fly that makes an appearance in the spring is the grannom sedge. It is supposed to hatch in April, but it doesn't know this. Sometimes on the Teme it hatches as early as mid-March in warm spring weather. It is a drab browny, grey little thing but easily recognized because when it hatches, it can hatch in its thousands. Clouds of these little sedges can sometimes be seen from the road which runs alongside the river at Little Hereford. The paradox is, that despite the numbers of fly, very few fish seem to rise to them. Repeatedly the notebook reads 'good hatch of grannom, no fish rising'.

In the warmer days of late April and early May, the hatch extends throughout the day. Following the grannom, the hawthorn fly is the next 'hatch'. The hawthorn fly does not hatch from the river; it emerges from the damp soil as the weather warms. They hang around the leeward side of riverside trees and hedges, fly-fishermen watch for clouds of these gangling black flies. When the wind catches them out, they tumble onto the water. The Ledwyche and the Cound Brook sometimes have a very heavy fall of hawthorn fly. When such a fall happens dozens of trout can be seen rising, and several fish can often be covered without moving.

When fishing in the early days of the season it is likely that no fish will be rising. At best the odd fish may rise just once, so wet-fly fished downstream is a reasonable choice. There are some who say wet-fly downstream is just 'chuck and chance', needing no skill, and that the way to fish wet-fly is upstream. Everyone is entitled to their opinion. If the fishery rules permit, downstream is a relaxed way of fishing that is often very productive.

Fishing downstream with a little wet-fly or nymph is a good way of exploring the river. Cast across and let the flies drift down in the current, sinking as they go. The fly's drift down often finds a fish feeding near the surface. Then, as the current begins to take hold, the flies lift and fish around in a curve that trout and grayling find irresistible. Care should be taken that you are in touch with your flies at all times when 'dead' drifting down the current. A tap on the rod tip or a lift of the bow in the line are indications of a trout taking the fly. This subtle and sensitive curve also allows the fly to be gently worked as it lifts and swings across the current.

There is a certain magic in working the fly across the stream, each knock and bump as a trout tweaks the fly is like an electric shock transmitted

Spring

along the line and through the rod. Of course sometimes the magic doesn't work but, in the spring with the sun shining and the whole season ahead of you, it is difficult not to be optimistic. Each ford and run must have trout in them, because didn't you fish them through those long winter nights and didn't a bright trout tug at the fly just at this very spot? You know as that fly swims across the current that it is inevitable that a take will come. Sure enough, the first trout of the season comes to meet the fly and in that moment all the waiting is over, it may not be big, but it is special, it's the first, and there will be many more to come.

AN OPENING DAY ON THE REA

If I had only one river to fish, obliged to spend the rest of my angling days on one stream, it would be the little River Rea. What is more, if confined to wander the banks of just one stretch, the choice without fail, would be where it ran through that loveliest part of Shropshire, around the crooked steeple of Cleobury Mortimer.

The Rea springs from the slopes of the Brown Clee; at well over a thousand feet it is the highest hill in Shropshire

Starting out from wild heather and bog, rivulets trickle down to meet brooks that meander through sheep grazed meadows and combine to form the Rea stream.

In case anyone is wondering, it is Ree as in sea, not Ray as in say. Evidence comes from the people of Cleobury, who have lived beside it for generations.

Once below Cleobury its character changes and coarse fish are found. As the Rea flows south through Neen Sollars amid soft rolling pastureland it slows further and after briefly forming the county boundary it passes out of Shropshire and into Worcestershire. At Newnham Bridge, it crosses the road from Birmingham, just in front of that splendid Victorian edifice, the Talbot Hotel. Here the angler escaping the city gets his first view of the water. A little further, and just out of sight of the road, it joins the Teme.

The little River Rea is typical of many lowland border streams. Like the Corve, Clun and Ledwyche, it is heavily wooded and flows mainly through pasture with small farms and few large estates.

The stretch above Cleobury is where trout reign supreme; the Rea here is just about perfect for a small river, constantly changing from shallow runs to deep pools. Alder trees line the banks and willows, beech, hazel and hawthorn add variety to the arcadian atmosphere. The blackthorn blossoms in early spring, looking like a drift of late snow, and if there is a little sun and warmth there will be a few spring olives hatching on the water around lunchtime.

Later in the year in Jolly June, when all is green and warm, it is nice to sit in the shade of the willow and watch for a rise. This stretch first gave a novice fly-fisher a trout back in the spring of eighty-five, more than a quarter of a century later, its charm remains.

Well, we have wandered its banks for long enough, let's go fishing! To start, we shall pick a day in early spring. The rain which had fallen unceasingly and the bitter east wind which had blown incessantly, stopped. For a few days the sun had been seen: it seemed spring had arrived. The beauty of these small trout streams is that with fair weather, and reasonable water levels, there is every chance of a few rising fish, even on the first day of the season. So, if you would care to read about it, here is a day from the diary.

The fishery is approached down a long farm drive. On this early spring day the car rolls past banks brightened by daffodils; 'that come before the swallow dares, and take the winds of March with beauty'. Once past a hillside copse the view opens out to reveal the valley of the Rea. The squat square church tower at Neen Savage can just be seen above the trees. Down in the valley the course of the river is revealed by the twisting line of trees with flashes of silver between. This is the view dreamt of during long winter evenings, when flies were dressed to tempt these springtime trout.

The car is parked outside the old farmhouse and Sugar, the resident cat, is here with a welcome. She looks happy and rolls over on the warm concrete path. It is always a good idea to start the season on a familiar water. Get the rods out of the car now, and watch the cat doesn't jump into the boot. A four weight, eight-foot rod is perfect, even a nine-foot rod will be suitable early in the season when the banks are clear.

It is eleven o'clock, when the clouds part, the weak spring sunshine warms the metal of the car. It gives hope of a hatch and the promise of a few rising fish by lunch. Time to pull on chestwaders and an old fishing jacket containing a fly box, floatant, tippet material, scissors, note pad, and a tape, that is all that is needed. No net: a net is a tedious thing.

The last thing to do before we set off is to straighten the leader. Using the rod tip, the end of the fly line is placed around a smooth fence post. Then holding the fly in one hand and the rod in the other, the nylon can be stretched. In this way coils caused by a winter on the reel can be drawn out.

We are ready to go, the farmhouse is mid-way along the fishery, today we will start from the downstream end. It is a short walk across the pasture to the river. A blustery breeze from the north sends a flight of rooks tumbling and wheeling across the grey sky. Lambs run to their mothers at the angler's approach, bunting the ewes for reassurance.

From the bank the water looks high but clear. The usual routine is to start at the downstream end and work up: on most of these small rivers an upstream approach is best. Walking down the water also gives a chance to spot any rises, then either to try a cast or mark them for later.

Today is typical for mid-March with the temperature struggling to get into double figures. A warm jacket is needed in order to be comfortable without restricting casting. A little sun would help things along and get a few flies hatching.

An Opening Day on the Rea

Now is the time to put into action wintertime plans, to exercise the rusty casting arm. It is good to start on the Rea, it is like meeting an old friend, and with a good head of fish it brightens the prospects for the day. In fishing the secret is finding fish; in spring it is finding feeding fish.

Sure enough, there is a rise in amongst the alder trees. Wait and watch, a dipper darts down the stream, there are no further rises; only twigs and last year's alder cones, blown loose by the breeze, stipple the surface. These fish are often 'oncers' remember the place and move on.

The start is the Rhubarb Patch, here in the summer is a patch of gunnera or giant green rhubarb. It is a favourite place to begin. The water here tails off into a shallow run where it is possible to work a wet-fly or nymph downstream and across the current.

Crouched down low to avoid spooking the trout, a Proustian moment, a smell so familiar, the smell of crushed vegetation and of river mud. A little line is fed out so the rod can roll it out; the size sixteen Option 2 drops with a tiny ring just short of the far bank. Raise the rod to straighten the line and keep in contact with the fly. Watch closely for any movement in the water. The tiny nymph swings around without incident. It feels good to be by the water again, rod in hand. Feed a little more line and roll the rod to flick the nymph further downstream, again gather in any slack and hold the rod high to guide the nymph across the stream. Twice more the fly searches the water without result. One more time and then the best area will have been covered, and knees stiff from crouching can be eased. Bang, a swirl and yank on the line. The trout, now gone, had struck at the nymph more in aggression than hunger, and fled. Nothing to be gained from carrying on there, the disturbed water means it's unlikely anything else will take.

Stand and stretch now and face upstream where a deep section has the look of a place likely to produce a fish. It would be better to see a rise, but we stirred a fish so they're still here. The same Option 2 is cast upstream now to sink into the deeper water and search out a fish. It is possible to watch the cast on the quieter water; it sinks but only slowly, pulling against the surface tension. It is not really fishing deep enough, swing it to hand, and have a look in the fly box. With nothing much on the water, try something general and nondescript, something that looks like food. A Gold Ribbed Hare's Ear pattern is a likely choice; it is weighted and dressed to look shrimp-like. Some people would tie on a gold-head fly of some sort, and that would work really well as an attractor pattern in this situation, but it is an attractor, a flashy gold thing, and not an imitation.

The size sixteen shrimp drops with a little splash mid-stream, the lead immediately takes it down towards the bottom and hopefully in front of a fish. Again slack is taken up and the rod raised to keep contact, the line hanging in a bow as the shrimp is brought back, just a fraction faster than the current. The rod is lifted and a loop thrown to lift the line into the air for the next cast. A side-cast, to miss the bankside bushes, puts the fly further up the stream. Let it sink, the nylon cutting down in a tiny 'vee' then lift and ever so slowly draw back. Again the fly searches the water, this can be slow work; believe each time the line will tighten as a fish takes hold, for to fish without belief is as pointless as fishing without a hook.

The next cast the fly sinks and then as if some force has taken it, speeds up, lift the rod and just like, that a trout is on. It is nice to feel the rod flexing again, coming alive in your hand, the rod tip stabbing down pointing out the trout as it battles for freedom. Below, a flash as the fish is brought to the surface and then he is splashing in the shallows. Hand line now, just a small fish, ten inches or so, but welcome on a difficult day. Grip his lower jaw and ease the barbless hook out. A moment to look now at this beautiful fish, the first of the season, then he speeds off back to the depths.

Well at least it's not a blank day; an empty creel is a heavy burden they used to say. It's gone midday, an hour spent in the pursuit of trout has passed in a moment.

Now is the best chance for a few rising fish; for the first time the smell of spring is in the air as the clouds part and the sun warms the earth. A fish on a dry fly would really round off the day. Back to the alders now where that fish rose earlier. A comfortable grass bank seat is chosen for its clear view up the river; time for a cup of coffee from the flask, and a chocolate bar from the pocket. It is good to take five minutes, watching the river, but nothing moves; only the bleating lambs, and a woodpigeon, startled by the visitor, clatters out of a grey ash tree.

Time is limited early season, if there is a rise it will be brief, so it is best to move on. There is a good spot a little further, here the river is more open, the spring sun can get on the water and warm the shallows. Small flies can be seen above the river, they are large dark olives, better named spring olives; they look quite light when flying against a dark background.

It is time to snip off the shrimp and select a dry fly, a little olive dun imitation. Called a Little Hereford in the notebook, it is nothing more than hare's ear fur body and CDC wing. On a size sixteen barbless hook, it is just the right size and that greyish brown colour to match the natural.

Out of the corner of the eye there is a movement, was it a rise? There again, further up and towards the far bank, rings reveal a rise. Opportunities rarely come knocking, they come quietly. Mark the spot by the clump of dry grass trailing into the water. Hook the little dun into the keeper ring and move up. Crouching low and following a narrow sheep trail down the bank to the water's edge, the target is now within range. Line is drawn out, and a 'warm up' cast is made to a likely place just short of the earlier rise. Nothing there, but it is worthwhile checking rather than 'line' a trout and see him arrow off. Another throw, this time the little dun lands lightly, floats cocked for a few seconds, before disappearing in the rings of a rise. The rod lifts and the line zips from the surface as the trout surprised leaps into the air. Once again that energy passes through the rod, a charge that passes to the hand, a connection with the wild trout now ploughing deep to gain sanctuary in the alder roots. The rod arches over, side-on to turn the fish, the flyline a streak of light disappearing into the depths. The rod's battle curve points to the stream now, maximum strain is used to hold the fish, and he turns, speeding downstream, leaving slack line trailing behind, a dangerous time, but luckily the hook hold is good and line is quickly stripped back through the rings, he's still on. Now it's more difficult fighting the trout against the current, and he's a good fish. He uses the weight of the water to add to his own, backing away from the pull of the rod, but he's weakening and by shifting position the rod once again applies pressure from below. Now the battle is over, the fish rolls on his side and the draw of the rod raises his head so he can be slid towards the bank. A firm grip on his lower jaw and the tape can be laid along his flank, fourteen inches, not the biggest, and no doubt on some waters considered rather small, but a good fish on a difficult day. He is returned with gratitude, maybe our paths will cross later in the season when the mayflies dance in the summer sun.

Now the sun has gone behind the clouds. Perhaps there would be a chance of another fish, but a chill breeze has sprung up and here will be more days to come. We are for home with a brace to record and that is a good result, a good day indeed.

A FISH FOR GOOD FRIDAY

This is an account of a spring day on the River Teme at Burford. Here the fast, shallow runs below the weir usually hold a few wild trout willing to come to the fly. It was the first outing of that season; the start had been delayed by wind, rain and high water until Good Friday. Then the day dawned with blue skies and a mild westerly which pushed along a scattering of clouds and promised the chance of some sport.

The car rolls down the lane, past Burford House, and is parked beside the lynch gate in front of the church. If you haven't seen inside Burford Church then you really should, it is probably the finest village church in the area. Today the service is at St Mary's, Tenbury, a mile downstream as the dipper flies.

Time to unpack the tackle. Everything has been checked and prepared over the winter months in anticipation of this very day. The fly-box is full, serried ranks carefully dressed and especially chosen for this moment. Now at last tackle is made up and the old familiar routine of checking pockets, mentally working through the sequence of line, tippet, flies and floatant is performed.

This stretch is the first of the Association's water upstream of Tenbury. Little has changed since it was founded in 1843. The section would have been well known to the Victorian angler arriving at the station and staying at the bow fronted Swan Hotel. From his window he could have looked out over the river. Then a short walk would bring him to the weir and its trout and shoals of grayling.

The river is still 'winter heavy'. Regular checks of the gauge at Tenbury have confirmed it is fishable but chestwaders and a wading staff will be needed.

Through the lynch gate and into the churchyard, the tattered remains of snowdrops under the trees give way to daffodils in hedge bottoms. Walking past the headstones, the angler may pass by an earlier member who has now crossed the river.

The path goes out through the 'kissing gate'. It has been used for a hundred years or more by anglers heading for the river. There, beneath the old apple trees, lambs in a frolic bounce in the spring grass and a buzzard flaps out of the trees to glide across the fields. It is a short walk to the river bank and the sturdy fisherman's stile which gives access to the weir. The old weir has a section removed to allow water and salmon through.

Over the winter a working party cleared trailing branches here. Then, in the cold, we sat back to admire our work over a flask of coffee and talked of the time when we would return to cast a fly. Now is the time to take advantage of our work. On the bank the bleached winter grasses are swept flat by recent floods. The water has cleared, yet the Teme is never entirely without colour. As anglers spend so much time considering the condition of water, it is surprising we don't have as many terms for it as the Inuit have for snow. Today it has the cold look of clear green glass. The shadows in the shallows show the brown stony bed while the flickering currents mirror the sky.

Standing on the old masonry of the weir, line is let out to be carried down the stream. Raise the rod, draw in a loop of line, and roll it out across the water. The line is lifted and straightened. The rod guides the line around, while the tip, held high, gently nods to the pull of the current. Step down, draw in and roll it out. This is wet-fly fishing: a gentle, relaxed and traditional way of catching trout.

As for flies, a March Hare and an Option 2 are tied on. The March Hare is just a hare's ear body with a game bird soft hackle. If dressed correctly it looks like a hatching nymph. It is usually attached as a dropper, or bob fly, and fished just beneath the surface. Then, on the point, the Option 2 imitates a swimming nymph; it anchors the pair so they do not skate across the surface, it also takes its share of fish.

The rod is carbon fibre, ten foot, casting a four weight line. It is longer than the usual nine foot 'river' rod. It was chosen to make it easier to work the fly across the stream.

The sun glints through the trees; it is not high in the sky so the steep bank on the Worcestershire side casts a chill shadow. Despite this spring olives are hatching, small flies ascending from the water, light coloured against the dark background. A grey wagtail dances across the stream to take a fly midair. He returns to perch on a rock, tail twitching. Later in April, he may nest near here

Move on down, step by step, casting all the time. By now the sun has warmed the water and more flies are rising over the river. Small greyish sedge flies are in the air drifting upstream, they are grannom sedges. The line goes out again. Given a touch of colour in the water, a gold bodied March Brown might have been the choice, or a Silver March Brown.

Familiar to anglers at Burford is the rock ridge which runs like a dorsal fin down the stream below the weir. With a heavy flow the crest of rock is submerged and strong currents run either side of it. Later in the season low water will leave it above the stream and it becomes a position from which to tackle the grayling. Now safety is paramount and the river here is best fished from the bank.

Again the line rolls out, the rod keeps up the rhythm, step down, draw in, and roll it out. Each cast fished out with the expectation of a strike. Every cast worked through, a free drift as the flies sink, lifting as the current catches hold, slackening or speeding as the rod bids. Below the surface the flies flit and flicker in the current; soft hackles waver in the water giving an impression of life.

The first part of the run has been covered, now the river widens and shallows. A gravel beach makes a shelf to wade on and gives a little more room for the back cast. Fishing here is usually good. It is also the best place to cross, but not today. Tug, midway across the river a fly gets a reaction. Just a tap, a tug, something alive: a promise of a fish.

The flies go out to cover the same section again, this time nothing. Sometimes the fish will come again. Try with a different angle, a different speed, still nothing.

Move on down, step by step, now casting with more confidence. When fishing with two flies there is always the thought as to which fly caught the fish's attention. Bang, again a strike, a boil in the water leaves a flat where a trout has risen to the fly but not held on. No doubt which fly he came to. Shorten the line a touch and cover the position again.

As always, contact is the key, work the flies into position, watch the line. Thump, this time the trout is firmly hooked. The rod is arched. The line is a streak against the dark water, signalling the location of the trout. He defies any attempt to control him. He must be a nice fish. Using the power of the stream he resists, kicking against the pull of the rod. A trout downstream, shaking his head against the hook, is always easy to lose. The rod maintains pressure; at any chance to gain ground the line is stripped in. Later in the season such a fish would be commonplace, today it is special; to lose him would be dire.

Now he is under control brought alongside but still not beaten. Joy at hooking becomes anguish in the struggle, an anxious time as he dives around waders and trailing line. Try to get his head up. He comes skating across the current, yellow flanks and white belly. His jaws are agape with the March Hare in the top of his mouth. Reach down and grasp his bottom jaw. No need to lift him from the water. He lies on his side in the current.

A moment to admire his olive back shading to golden yellow flanks spotted with bright red. A wild creature held captive for an instant before the little hook is slipped out and he is free again. The notebook records '9" March Hare below rock' but the first fish of the season is so much more. It is a promise of trout to come, a harbinger.

Time now to get line back onto the reel and check the tippet, the flies, check everything is in order. Survey the water, there are still a few spring olives hatching and flickering into the air.

Below the weir there is a long fast run. Here the water is broken and each rill and riffle look as if they may hold a trout. With rod and staff for comfort, a position is found at the head of this wide stream. From here an easy cast will cover the far bank and the rod will lead the fly across the noses of the trout. The need for a wading staff becomes quickly apparent: the sandstone is scoured with deep gouges down the river. It is very easy to stumble here. The nearside bank is thickly wooded, thus the need to wade. In the spring, on the bank above where the river flows, the celandines flower and the wild garlic grows.

A gentle cast sends the line looping out across the stream and the flies drop just short of the far bank. The rod is lifted and the line straightened with a mend, so immediately the flies are in contact and swimming effectively. Then as the line comes across, a movement? Something seemed to flash amongst the flickering, sparkling waters.

Another cast goes out, shorten the line and bring it across the same spot. Yes! A take confirms a fish was there. This time the fight is less dashing more a tug, tug, as the fish fights stubborn and holds deep. A grayling; soon a small silver fish is sliding across the surface towards the waiting hand. He returns with a pact to meet again in the autumn.

The day continues into the afternoon as these angling days are apt to, with a tug of a hidden fish that remains hidden, the zip of a dipper flying by and the occasional fish that comes off the hook. The bright sun of the morning is hidden now behind the tall trees and fewer flies are to be seen. It is towards the end of the run, one large alder stands out on the far bank, its mossy roots a haven for a trout.

By now the casting arm has its rhythm and the line rolls out to land the flies under the alder tree.

A Fish for Good Friday

Once, twice, a third time the likely lie is searched. Then slam, a fish strikes hard as the flies swing across the stream. The rod tip is hauled over as a good-sized trout heads off towards Tenbury. Let the loose line out carefully, no jerking that could cause the hook to pull out. Reel in the slack. Now he can be played straight from the reel; a palm cupped on the rim acts as a brake if he should run again. He is still deep, good; if he thrashes on the surface he may throw the hook. The plan is to walk down to him reeling in and shortening the line as we go. He remains still, just a heavy force on the bed of the river. Alongside now, he feels the change in the pull of the line and tries to run upstream. He's fighting the current and the drag of the line. His mouth is tight closed, the hook pulled well into his jaw. He tires and tumbles down to twist and fight under the rod tip. Keep his head up. He's a good fish but he's beaten now, caught by the Option 2 in the tip of his jaw. With the line taut, the March Hare dangles above the water. Just strength for one more dive against the pull of the line and then he rolls on his side and is quickly brought, head up, within reach.

He deserves the honour of the tape. Held firm by lower jaw the tape is draped along his flank. Cradled head into the flow he spreads his fins and pushes off strongly into the current. For a moment he lies on the stream bed, gills opening, then is gone. He goes into the note book, '15" Option 2 B'ford weir run'. A good fish for any time of the year and a good fish to end on; for this is the end of the run and time has flown as it does by the waterside.

Take a moment to take in the river, the trees, a flash of a dipper heading upstream. Time to listen again to the water's music, heard since time immemorial by those who come to the riverside. Ghosts? No, this river bank is not haunted: only haunting, for though we must leave the river, the river never leaves us.

Walking the path back to the car, a chill wind rakes through the trees and the sun is hidden behind leaden clouds. Perhaps today was a lone sunny day, a false spring; no matter, the days will lengthen, the weak sun will get stronger, and we will be back by the river to find out what the rest of the season holds.

SUMMER

In the Teme valley, after the spring months have passed, there follows several months of the best trout fishing the angler is likely to experience. The angler's summer starts with the mayfly. Some old fishers start their season with the mayfly, saying that it brings the fish up. It can certainly be the best fishing of the year, but do not miss the early season sport.

The mayfly hatch gets under way regularly each year in mid-May. At first the advanced guard comes in ones and twos, then comes heavier hatches at the end of the month. On border streams these early flies will be small, probably males, about a size fourteen in hook size. The larger female duns and spinners are nearer size twelve. Many patterns from books recommend much larger sizes. It could be our border mayfly are smaller than their chalk-stream cousins. Large mayfly patterns are difficult to cast, twist the tippet, and are poor hookers of trout. Try, as ever, to match what you see on the water.

Early May can be a quiet time for anyone waiting for a rise; many trout may feed on mayfly nymphs as they prepare to hatch. Early in May, a nymph imitation can save a blank day; later during the hatch, a nymph fished in the surface will take fish. One of the wonderful things an angler sees is a mayfly hatching from its case; scoop one up and it will happen in your hand, magical.

Mayfly time can be thrilling, casting large flies to (hopefully) large trout. Abundance has returned. Trout, which have a lean time most of the year can feast; for the angler too, it is a time of plenty.

It could be that for the first time the angler can sit on a warm dry grass bank and relax. The chill winds of spring are gone, replaced by a warm breeze. The days grow longer, pigeons coo in shading trees, 'take two cows, taffy take two'. Calm comes to the river.

In the borderlands, mayfly hatch in large numbers from late May to late June but continue hatching into August. A Mayfly pattern will take fish on border streams throughout this period. At the start of mayfly time the trout will feed heavily on nymphs; at the end they focus on spinners. A spent pattern fished in an eddy is likely to tempt a hefty trout.

It has been said that trout fill up on mayfly and do not feed in the following month. A trout is a very simple animal, its gut a short tube, it seems unlikely that it would not be able to feed very shortly after the mayfly feast. Although the mayfly festival may have passed, border stream trout will feed throughout the summer.

By mid-summer, the light is holding into late evening; on warm days the rise can go on until it is too dark to see. Other evenings the rise can switch off as bats start to flit up the stream.

On warm summer evenings expect a hatch of just about every upwinged fly in the book. Mayfly, yellow may dun, blue-winged olives, pale wateries, small dark olives, gnats and sedge flies of all sorts can fill the air in a floating soup.

Now is the time for fine tackle, a treasured cane rod, an old Hardy reel, a light line, and a size eighteen spent olive. It is a time for finesse after the solid tackle of mayfly time. Individual trout are targeted. To match not only the fly, but also the stage at which it is being taken, is a test for the angler's ability. This is close one-to-one fishing with an emphasis on technique, changing flies to find the correct size, colour, and attitude.

It can be technical fishing, when trout after trout is taken, - once the right choice is found. Trout hover on the fin sipping flies as they drift down, precision is key, aim to float it between his eyes. It is great fun when having swapped flies several times over a persistent riser, to finally deceive it at close range with a diminutive nymph fished in the surface on a fine tippet, and have a fighting sixteen inch wild trout burst out of its lie and take line as it dashes across the stream.

Never quit before the evening rise. Anglers, who have travelled far to fish an unfamiliar border river, can spend all day flogging away with little reward, especially in the heat of summer. They leave discouraged and disillusioned, saying the water was not what they had hoped for. If only they had stayed into the evening they would have found the reluctant fish far more receptive at the end of the day. At dusk they may have more chances in two hours than they had in the rest of their day; so always stay for the evening rise.

Fortunately, high summer has less effect on the border streams than on some southern streams. On small Shropshire streams there are few 'dog days' when all fish lie unmoving.

The trout of the Teme valley rise under their dark tunnels of trees, on even the warmest days one can almost certainly be found to rise to a carefully presented black gnat.

Low water is the problem here if we have a summer drought. Streams drop to low levels and slow to a trickle; trout hide in such exposed conditions. Then the best, if not the only, fishing is in the evening.

Sometime, as high summer passes, there will come a touch of autumn in the air; the fruits are ripening in the orchard and the nights begin to draw in. Then the angler's thoughts will turn to grayling.

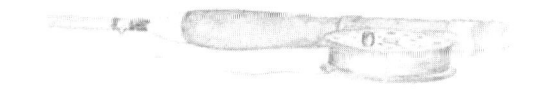

BY ONNY

I suppose the title should read 'By Ony' if we were to follow the poets lead, for the little River Onny runs through his 'land of lost content'.

A. E. Housman's poetry, simple and perfect, reflects these little rivers with their simple beauty. However, we shall stay with the main stream and 'By Onny' it shall be.

The River Onny is a delightful stream. Like many border streams it starts on the high open hills, gathering in dingles, forming brooks in the little valleys between the wooded hillsides, before tumbling down to the rich pastures of the dale.

The River Onny starts as two main branches, the West Onny and East Onny. Their watershed is the Long Mynd and its surrounding hills. The branches join above Craven Arms, the only town by which it flows.

Craven Arms may sound like a public house but it is a border town formed at the junction of the A49 (Watling Street) and the roads from Clun and Bishops Castle to the west and Much Wenlock and

Bridgnorth to the east. With good access from four points of the compass and a main railway line it became a busy station and livestock market. Today the market, that once dominated the centre of the town, has gone and the station is much reduced.

Nowadays shops and cafes welcome visitors, but the no-nonsense character of the drovers still remains in 'The Arms', as the locals call it. Although not as pretty or genteel as its neighbours, Church Stretton and Ludlow, it is surrounded by some of the finest scenery in Shropshire.

Historically the Onny was one of the waters fished by the Rev. Powell of 'Orange Otter' fame. He lived up the road at Munslow and would have been familiar with the Onny as he crossed it just outside of Craven Arms, near the hamlet of Halford.

Below Craven Arms the character of the Onny changes, it runs through a wide valley which it shares with the A49 and the main Hereford to Shrewsbury rail line. Anglers travelling by are treated to glimpses of the river, more open here and with wide gravelly bends and steep clay banks. It meets the Teme just north of Ludlow in the village of Bromfield.

Access to much of the Onny is difficult. It flows through large estates and the fishing clubs and associations are few and exclusive. Hopefully more sections will become available in the future. One section that is available to fish will be known to many anglers. Just a ten minute walk from the town, it starts at the bridge carrying the road to Much Wenlock. This is the section once held by the mighty Birmingham Anglers Association and it was a favourite destination for the gamefisher escaping from the urban sprawl of Birmingham. Here, many novice anglers had their first taste of wild trout fishing. It was wonderful to leave the grey city behind, to enter into, by degrees, the green of the Welsh borderlands, to breathe the fresh country air and listen to birds and sheep rather than the factory racket.

A few years ago it was possible to fish the stretch for three pounds a day. Indeed it formed part of the trinity 'Onny, Teme and Clun', that could be fished in a day for a total costs of four pounds with the expectation of a brace of trout from each. The Onny here runs through open pasture, grazed by cattle. The river holds a good head of trout and grayling as well as chub, fished for with float and fly.

The water is still available on a day ticket as I write, though it costs a little more, you may only use the fly, and woe betide anyone taking a trout home for tea. Times change and it may be necessary to control fishing more strictly, but I hope these waters will not be too tightly regulated. Here is a day from the diary, from a less restrictive time, when the angler could go the waterside equipped with whichever rod was appropriate to the quarry and the season.

BY ONNY WITH FLY

An evening by the Onny, this time with the fly rod, with the aim of catching the Onny's yellow flanked wild trout. Dry weather means the river is low, but it is a warm evening and there should be flies hatching and trout rising.

The car is parked and tackle assembled. Then it is only a short walk down to the river. Today the start is at the run into the bridge pool, a favourite place for grayling in the autumn, now likely to hold a trout or two in the fast water. To get to the spot entails climbing over a sagging barbed wire fence, then a crouching, bent-over walk down the bank to the waterside. Anglers who fish these open streams will know the walk, trying to be as small as possible while pretending to be invisible. Hopefully not having spooked the fish the tackle is readied.

An eight-foot split-cane rod is just long enough to cover the little river, a rod a little longer would do as well on these open banks. A light line, probably a four or five weight is ideal, precision taking precedence over power. Now opening the fly box, a little Hare's Ear is chosen to mimic the little olives that are dancing over the water. A size sixteen looks about right and is tied to three pound breaking-strain nylon. The fly is given a light rub of grease to ensure it floats.

Flexing the rod works a little line out, the line slides through the rings and tugs the fly held loosely between thumb and finger, let go and a soft looping cast lands the fly at the tail of the run.

Now pick up and roll the line forward, searching the water. Push on a little further upstream into those creases where a rise would be expected.

A rise, further up near the head of the run, mark that for later. Surprising how rises are seen when you are focused on the water. To a trout that slower water just to the side of the main stream would be a good place. The fly lands in the crease between the two, enticing any trout to rise, nothing. Try again, in the gentle water, with slack line to stop the drag, bang. He went for it just as the drag set in, must have pulled it from his mouth. Lift, roll, cast. Try one down the main current.

The fly lands in the fast, broken flow, floats over a window of glassy clear water before getting lost in the jumble of light. Another rise, a splash in the rapid water, gives confidence. Cover the rise and yes. Lift the rod and a surprised and angry trout comes tumbling down the stream. He scoots across the current. Having gained his wits he fights like a fish twice his size, stubborn twists and turns until he comes head up skated across the surface to the waiting hand. A quick check to confirm he is a trout not a salmon parr shows the red spot of a trout on the edge of his adipose fin. A twist of the barbless hook and he slips free and is immediately lost in the flickering shadows and mirrors of the stream. Make a note in the book, dry the fly, a touch of grease, and work the line back out.

Half way up now, in reach of the rising fish at the head of the run. Rhythm and timing, the line curling out and, with a flick, dropping the Hare's Ear on the water. Work both sides of the current, dropping it onto any calm water, a splash, the fly is gone. The line tightens as a trout snatches the fly and dives upstream. Rod tip up, the line shows where the trout is trying to hold himself in the fast water. He loses balance and drops downstream, strip in line now, to keep in contact, and he's gone. Loose line trails in the stream. Oh well, it happens. Probably this run is finished. No, another rise, and pretty much in the same place. These runs hold quite a few of these little trout, fin by fin. Again float the fly over the spot, and straight away it is taken. The rod tip goes up and a tiny trout comes helter-skelter down the run. Perfect trout in miniature, he drops off the hook as he is lifted from the water, and scoots back to his lie. It is time to move on.

Upstream now, past where the river bends and twists between alders and hawthorns. This is the haunt of chub. When autumn comes, trotting a float under the overhanging branches may bring the reward of a brass-scaled fish. The chub are not big, but they are the biggest fish in the river until the salmon run up on the winter floods. Now it is the wild trout that are the target.

There are two rising where the river swings around in a big bend. It's an awkward cast from a muddy cattle drink to the nearest fish set tight against the rocks of the far bank. The first cast, just a sighter, falls mid-stream and short. The second better, but still not close enough to the bank. Another rise, again tight to the bank, gives something to aim for. A cast in reply drops the fly just right, but it is quickly dragged away by the current. No wonder the trout has taken up station there. The quicker current brings food, and the slower, against the rock-side, gives him a calm place to lie.

Maybe a better angle would give a drift, even if it is just a short one. A bent kneed walk upstream improves the angle, more directly across the flow. The fly hits the far bank rocks, and drops lightly down, tight to the bank. A tiny dimple and the fly is sucked in. Contact, swing the rod hard over, it jerks as the trout fights downstream. He uses the current, twisting with all his strength, resisting the pull of the line. Stumbling as mud grips waders, control is regained. He tires now and comes to hand. A handsome spotted fish, unhooked, held for a moment, head into current, gills working, then he's gone. The note in the book says '12" GRHE #16'.

Now pause and watch the pool. Check the fly, it is waterlogged and muddy, a change is needed. Since the start there have been olives hatching, a Little Hereford should do the job. It is a similar fly to the Hare's Ear, but with a wing of Cul de Canard, it looks more like an olive dun. Text books say watch the hatching duns as they float down to check the species; on these broken waters it is seldom possible.

There, further up and more to mid-stream, a rise. The size sixteen Little Hereford is tied on ready to cover the fish. He rises again. A slow, easy cast drops the fly just ahead of the last rise. The dense wing is easily seen amongst the reflections as it dances back down the stream. Rise, he's on, again the rod tip bends to point out the trout struggling in the current. There is always an electric thrill as the rod comes alive. This fellow is game, but no giant, he comes wallowing through the shallows. Turn the hook and he's away. '9" LH #16' says the note book.

There are many corners on this stretch of the Onny: it would take a day to fish them all. That stump washed down in the winter flood looks a good lie, but time is pressing so it is left for another day.

The next pool is long and slow, there are rises at the tail, but by the number and frequency they are pinks, immature grayling of around six inches. In the deeper water upstream, there is a rise. It looks more promising, so the fly is sent to land gently by the far bank. The Little Hereford floats over the spot where the fish rose, he rises again, further upstream. One more cast, again the fly lands on target, again it is ignored, more pinks. Much time can be wasted on pinks.

A careful wade brings the far bank willow within range. There is a rise just short of the branches, a cast drops the fly on target and immediately a rise, but the fly is still there. Pick up, roll, and drop the fly back on the spot, again a rise. Lift the rod, but it is evident the fish is only playing with the fly, another pink. Sometimes adult grayling act this way, possibly taking tiny flies or 'smutting', more often it is pinks. Time to hook the little dun into the keeper ring and move on.

Moving upstream there is a broad ford usually well weeded in the summer. It is a good spawning place for the coarse fish to lay their eggs. Perhaps there are small trout amongst the mat of weed but it's very difficult to get a fly to them.

The Onny is one of the few border rivers that often produces good growth of water weed, usually Ranunculus, the water crowfoot. However, as in other streams, growth is unreliable, being easily washed out in winter floods. These are nothing like the managed weedbeds of the chalk-streams. Weedbeds on border rivers are valued and encouraged as spawning sites, shelter and producers of food. Possibly the want of roach, dace, and perch on the Teme is due to the loss of suitable weed for spawning.

On the Onny, the character of the stream hereabouts is similar to the Wye's vale where open banks and gravel bottoms are more common. This next pool is exposed, to avoid the skyline a good ploy is to drop in at the tail and work up. Sliding down the bank, the water flows under the rod arm, a comfortable position for the right-handed angler. Usually at the tail there is a shoal of grayling. Today, in summer, the only fish are more pinks. At this point it is a good idea to sit and watch for a rise. There were olives hatching earlier, now closer to the level of the water they can be more easily seen. A few have not fully hatched and are sprawled flat in the surface film. In the fly box a spinner pattern stands out, a size sixteen olive dressed spent. It has the size, colour, and importantly, same pose as the naturals. There are rises at the head of the pool, but there are trout all the way up, so moving up would alarm them. Now is the time to wait and see if another shows closer to hand. Maybe use the 'three rise rule', if there are three or more rises further upstream, move up.

One of the features of this stretch of the river is that it has a public footpath running alongside it. Some anglers dislike having people around. It can be annoying to have people tell you they wouldn't have the patience to fish, and then spend ages watching you. This time a couple of lads come walking up the river carrying rods, with little silver spinners tinkling against the butt. The usual greeting is met with silence. Then one says in very broken English 'Feeshing'. Anglers the world over have this in common. With grins and a lot of hand waving we wish each other 'Good luck' and they carry on their way. International relations take a step forward. Given the heat and the low water, I would have bet on my spinner, against theirs, to produce a fish today.

As they walk off, a fish rises, not quite within range but close enough to encourage a little shuffle forward. Line is worked out and a gentle cast made to get the range, a rise, but just a grayling pink playing with the fly. There, close into the bank a solid rise. No splash, just a heave as the top of his head breaks through, characteristic of a trout feeding close to the surface.

A careful cast is needed; the fly is swept forward to land softly in front of his nose and floats down over the spot, where the trout ignores it. Allow it to fish down, well out of range, and lift and roll forward. This time the cast is a little askew and the fly lands very close to the trailing brambles.

The flow is slower tight into the bank and the fly is held back while the leader is drawn away. Just as it is about to drag, that confident rise again. The rod tip goes up and battle is joined. Trout here do not usually grow large, but this fellow powers up the stream putting a fair bend in the rod. Swing the rod over now to stop him surging upstream and disturbing the others. The rod is level with the water, bending into a full fighting curve. The strain is too much and the trout tumbles back downstream. Line is stripped back to keep in touch, and he is held close in. He still fights to get downstream, but he's fired his best shots. His head is up and grasping the tippet he is brought in, the little spinner clipped in the corner of his jaw. Swiftly unhooked and admired, yellow sides with bright red spots, a real beauty, about twelve inches, a good fish in every way.

Time to sort things out. A note is made in the book. Line is wound back on the reel. Check the nylon. Examine the fly, hackle preened, dried and greased. Hopefully the fish at the top of the pool have not been disturbed. No, there. As the stream runs through the weed at the head of the pool, a rise in the trailing fronds.

It is difficult to edge forward along the waterline without slipping in and sending a bow wave up the pool. So crouch low and edge along the bank top, pretend to be a sheep until there is a place to slide back down to water level.

Of course, if there are dog walkers strolling along the riverside path, no doubt they think you have gone mad. It can be galling to have them walk up and peer over the top to see what you were crawling up to. This time the dog walkers stay clear and the trout continue to rise.

There are at least two fish rising. One is midstream at the trailing edge of the weed, and one close in to the bank in the main flow. The one in the better lie of deep water close to the bank is probably the better fish. The little spinner is unhitched from the keeper ring and enough line worked out to cover the target.

Another rise, the rod flexes and sends the trout a line. Reaching its target the fly settles down on the water amongst the foam and debris of the feeding line. Swirling around in the current there is a dimple and the fly is gone. Again the rod lifts in response and the satisfying thump of a good fish is the answer. This fellow cannot be stopped from ripping across the pool, as long as he does not entangle himself in the weed, we are okay. A streak of light shows the connection with the trout, the stripe of fly line pointing out were the trout is trying to gain sanctuary under the weed. The split-cane rod comes to life with a lively wild trout attached to it. The trout, thwarted from gaining the weeds, swings over towards the roots and brambles trailing into the water. Line is stripped back to keep contact; the bend in the rod absorbs the plunges of the fish, the nylon is stretched taut. He must be held at all costs. Then he is in open water, now he can be beaten. No need for concealment now, taking to the water makes it easier to bring him to hand and unhook. A gallant fish that deserves the recognition of the tape, fourteen inches, one of the best from here, and a notable fish in the diary. The little spent olive fly is retired to the fly patch, a good pattern, but no name, the notebook reads 'Mepps' Spinner #16.

THE RIVER CORVE

The River Corve is a difficult river. It gives its name to one of the most beautiful areas of Shropshire, the Corve Dale, and to one of the most important streets in Ludlow, Corve Street.

However the river itself is somewhat disappointing. At the top of the dale it is little more than a trickle and by the time it passes Munslow, the home of the late Rev. Edward Powell, it is no more than a small brook. It is only when it reaches Diddlebury that it becomes a stream of any size.

For a twelve-year-old boy with an old bicycle the Corve was an irresistible attraction and where it crossed the road to Diddlebury there was a bridge with white railings. The summer air is chilly at five in the morning, the time all good anglers were supposed to start, according to popular advice. It was mainly downhill for the five mile trip, past sleeping cottages and farms just waking. Rods strapped to the crossbar, through the chill air in hollows - even in June, with wellingtons and streaming eyes he flew. The bike was lent against the railings and then it was down the bank always to the same spot under the road bridge. Anglers are inveterate bridge leaners and know there is usually a 'Bridge Pool' and here was no different. A short glass-fibre rod was set up and a worm sent out to lure any trout gullible enough to fall for the trap. A few were, until these early morning excursions were brought to an abrupt halt by the local gamekeeper. Enough said. Any angler crossing the same bridge will find the same stream, now strangely smaller.

As the Corve flows down its dale it loses some of its sparkle. The land flattens, the river proceeds at a leisurely pace and deepens, so much so that once, crossing the river by Stanton Lacy, my horse had to swim. It passes by the racecourse before winding around the northern outskirts of Ludlow.

Here, at the bottom of Corve Street in the floods of 2007 it washed away the bridge and half a house. The lovely old stone bridge was replaced by a concrete slab, but park there and you will see some of the Corve at its best. Its flows quickens

The River Corve

around the slopes of Ludlow and it enters the Teme an arrow's flight from the Castle.

It is this tail end that most anglers will have fished. At one time it was under the control of the Ludlow Angling Club, along with the stretch of the Teme upstream which included some splendid grayling runs. Alas, to my knowledge, it is no longer available, hopefully it may be in the future and anglers able to fish it again. This is a problem on the Corve, access is very limited. Farmers and landowners may give permission and it would be worthwhile selecting a suitable stretch and trying it. While this last half mile of the Corve was accessible for members of the Ludlow Angling Club it featured regularly in the diary. Here is one such day.

This tail end of the Corve is just a twenty minute walk from Ludlow town centre. A public footpath leads off a lane and to a bridge which is the first sight of the water. A pause here to take in the river, look for rises, look for flies, just look.

Upstream the river winds between alders with a few clear spaces where anglers have worn the grass down. It looks worth a stroll to see if anything can be found rising. There in a tunnel of alders, a rise. The 'pitches' or 'pegs' formed by the anglers give a clear run downstream, to benefit those trotting a float. This is little help to the dry fly man. Try to attack him from downstream, no, thick vegetation and trailing trees prevent a cast even with the shortest of rods. Further upstream the trees are closer together, the water shallows and looks more 'trouty' but trailing and fallen branches bar the way. Time to head downstream. To start at the bottom of a stretch and work upstream is always a good plan.

The downstream end of this fishery is its confluence with the Teme. Here the Corve deepens, held back by the flow of the main river. Curiosity leads to a walk down to this point, what lover of rivers can resist finding the point where they start, or finish? No trout fishing here; deep, still water is bordered by alders. Here also the pitches have been numbered as 'pegs' to be used in a match if needed. A good example of a backwater where fish may gather in winter floods, but not what is called for today.

Further upstream there was a section with open banks and a bend, and on an unfamiliar river and with difficult conditions, go for the easy option. Here the river had washed a beach on the inside and formed a clay 'cliff' on the outside; clear of trees it would at least be easy to fish. A comfortable place is found to settle at the tail of this run and take a break.

It is a hot day, trying to fish thus far has been frustrating, time to slip the jacket off, suck a sweet and watch the water. There, a kingfisher darting downstream alights on a dead alder branch. He sits still, the branch bobs him up and down. Has he a nest in the clay bank opposite? No sign of a nest-hole, he darts back upstream leaving the little branch bouncing. Calm is restored, the water has cooled hot temper as it always does and now the angler is in harmony with the river.

A rise, in the fast, deep run close to the bank. Check tackle, angry or careless casting often leads to wind-knots and tangles. All is clear this time, but the fly which was a bushy Alder is swapped for a little size sixteen Light Olive.

Another rise this time close to, at the tail of the pool. Wind in a little line and a gentle easy cast flicks the fly into position, it is gone. The rod goes up and a wick little fish comes back down through the shallows, a parr. He is quickly unhooked and darts back to safety. Parr are thick in the shallows of the Corve and Teme around Ludlow.

Check and dry the fly. Watch for a rise, there against the high bankside. Shift position slightly to ensure the cast doesn't drag too soon. Short casts are best. Now check behind and a gentle flip lands the fly in the stream where it floats back down amongst the flecks of foam. It's gone, in a blink the fly disappears and the rod tip goes up. This time there is a satisfying weight on the end of the line. Not gigantic by any means, the line quivers in the current as the trout pushes upstream, and then he is drawn back down to kick and fight in the shallows. Run a hand down the line to hold him fast. Once the line is touched I count the fish caught, for the next move is to unhook him, (I believe the rule is applied in Marlin fishing). He is held for a moment, side on in the current, silvery flanks and light olive brown dappled with the red spots of a brown trout.

All trout are unique. Once released he arrows away into the stream. At last a fish to record in the notebook, as for size? The diary tells me ten inches, but it matters not.

Now sit back, and watch for another rise. The kingfisher darts downstream without stopping. There, towards the top of the run, a tiny splash amid the tumble of the stream. The fly is readied and with a flick sent out to ask the question. First time down there is no reply. Send it out again. It lands lightly on hackle tips and skips back down the stream. Another rise, to an unseen natural fly, it is difficult on these small streams to spot flies especially on fast broken water. He's seen the Little Olive, time to show him something different. The fly box has an assortment of patterns and sizes. A little Black Gnat might work; if in doubt use something small and dark. The little Gnat is sent out, a black speck it floats, and is gone. The rod tip lifts line to contact trout number two. He holds in the stream, the rod bent to the pull of the fish. He feels a stronger fish, he kicks and rolls in the current, but the stream is against him and he falls back under pressure from the rod. Quickly, get his head up and unhook him; An inch bigger than the first perhaps, he too is returned to his home.

In truth, the only section of interest to the fly-fisherman that was open enough to fish, was that corner run. Now, since the floods, debris has been cleared and the last few fields of the Corve are better maintained but who fishes there, I don't know. My tale ends with a brace of trout on what was a difficult day on a difficult river.

THE CLUN RIVER

The little river Clun rises on the Welsh border. It wanders through West Shropshire passing through Clun, Clunton, Clunbury, and Clungunford, the villages the poet said 'are the quietest under the sun', few would argue.

As far upstream as Clun the river holds both trout and a good head of grayling, which is unusual for such a small stream: then strange things do happen in Clun.

Here is a trip to the Clun in June from the diary. There is no urgency getting to the river. Most of the country has been sweltering in temperatures hovering around thirty degrees. Fishing in the heat of the day would have been frustrating, now after tea, the glare of the sun is less. It will be a blessed relief to get into the cool water under the shade of the trees.

The tranquil town of Clun drowses in the folds of the border hills. The river runs through the town, today it runs only slowly; 'Low and clear', is the note in the diary. With the summer vegetation at its highest, access will be by wading; chestwaders and a short rod will be needed.

It is just a short walk to the river. The first pool is a deep bend. Drop onto the gravel at the tail of the pool, and happily, there is a rise just within range. This pool is a classic drag trap, deeper slow water in the pool, faster water in the shallow tail. The usual tactic is to cast a small nymph upstream; an Option Two is tied on, a size sixteen nymph, small but heavy. A cast drops it into the slower water where the trout rose. There is enough slack in the leader to allow the nymph to sink. Holding the line up off the water maintains a drag free drift. The line starts to tighten as the current takes hold and the nymph rises in the water. Just as the cast is fished out and line is drawn in to prepare for the next cast, the line stops. Usually it is simply the nymph catching bottom as it trundles over the shallows. This time a lift of the rod is met with live resistance. The resistance is an eight inch trout that was holding in the tail of the pool. Quickly he is brought to a wet hand and cradled just long enough to admire his bright red spots and golden yellow flanks.

Of all the streams and rivers in the valley, surely the Clun produces the most beautiful trout. One Clun trout was so spotted that every surface was covered with red spots, head, tail, and fins. The bright red spots on its body were set on an intense yellow and vivid olive-green background. It was a little jewel. The most brightly coloured brown trout I have ever seen. Perhaps it was mutation or deviation for it is doubtful if such a colourful aberration would survive long among predators. I only wish I had photographed it for I have never seen anything like it since.

The next cast brings no result. It is time to wade further upstream into the pool. Another cast, but the little nymph fishes through with no result. Although there were no tell tail bow waves as a trout arrowed out of its lie, it is likely the small trout in the shallows have moved into the deeper pool, disturbing the rest of the fish. It is possible to wade carefully upstream, edging forward and tucking into the near bank, to be in range of the head of the pool. There the river runs fast under a footbridge, as the current flows along the far bank, there is a rise. This is a classic spot for a trout and a second fish rises to confirm it. It is not clear what these fish are rising to; there are no duns on the water, in the air only midges show against the sky.

Trout in small streams rise freely. They rise whenever there is any chance of food on the surface. Usually it is little black bugs and beetles, which have fallen in that attract their attention. If the trout are looking up it is always worthwhile trying a general dry fly pattern. In view of that, a lightly greased Black Gnat, size sixteen is tied on. Cast to land softly at the head of the run, it floats down before starting to swing into the slower current of the pool. The rod is raised to take line off the water to reduce the chance of drag, a rise, and a miss.

Sometimes it happens that way. The fly coming back downstream, a short rod and too much slack line, means a fish can take and reject the fly before the rod makes contact. Oh well, at least they are rising. The fly is checked and despatched to alight again at the head of the pool.

The Clun River

This time it is the upstream fish that rises and takes the fly, no hesitation this time as the line tightens on a lively trout. The fish dashes around the pool putting a fine bend into the rod. The pressure soon tells and he is brought to the bank. A quick estimate, nine inches, and a note of its fine condition, white leading edge to its fins, is made before he swims back to the depths. The little Black Gnat is swilled off in the water and dried on a piece of tissue, but no more trout rise in this pool. Time to wade further upstream.

The Clun, upstream of Clun town, is only a small river. It has few nasty surprises by way of rock ledges, as the Teme has. However it can get quite deep, be prepared, when wading use chestwaders, thighwaders are often not enough. Many of these small rivers such as the Clun, Onny, Ledwyche, Rea, and Corve, are easier to fish while wading. The difficulty of fishing from the banks is that they are often lined with trees and vegetation so dense that it is impossible to swing a rod. The other problem is due to the incised nature of the rivers the water level is usually much lower than the bank top. Frequently there is a six to ten foot drop down the bank. The banks are often too steep to stand on, and descend straight into the water. The riverbed on the other hand is relatively level and the tunnel under the overhanging branches is sometimes the only clear space.

Wading upstream, the next pool starts at the footbridge. This long narrow stretch holds a grayling shoal throughout the year, along with a few trout. A rise, just upstream of the bridge. The little Black Gnat is unhooked from the keeper ring and flicked ahead to cover the rise, no response. A tricky spot this, tight between alders on both banks, twigs snatch at the fly on the back cast. Cast again, no response, and the fly can no longer be seen, it may be waterlogged or have snapped off. Time to check before continuing fishing, you seldom get a fish on a sunken dry-fly, and never if it's not there. A curl of nylon is the only thing at the end of the line.

Open the fly box and select a replacement, a fly that catches the eye is a trial pattern based on a green and partridge, dressed after catching some trout from this stretch that had been feeding on

The Clun River

green-fly. It is tied on and sent out to land lightly, just ahead of the rise. It fishes just below the surface, a movement under water, and a fish is on. This little fellow zips across the pool, the rod tangles with branches and there is a fine mess of knitting before he is under control and can be brought to hand. A lovely heavily spotted trout of around eight inches. Now time to sort out the cast before moving on.

Again, a rise and again the green-fly lands ahead of the rise, another fish, this time diving deep with a tug-tug of a grayling. Soon the silver gleam confirms a nice grayling in splendid condition, he fights until he is brought to hand, and slipped off the hook.

Towards the top of the pool there is a good rise, again a stealthy wade is needed to come within range. There is a bend with the water swinging across to the near bank below a hawthorn bush. The rise was in this main flow, the thalweg, which is marked by the stream of bubbles or foam. Trout often hold in this main flow into the pool, except where it is too fast and turbulent, when they'll hold to the side of it; the simple reason being, a lot of food is being washed down by the current.

As expected, another rise breaks the surface in amongst the froth. The soft hackle fly would be difficult to follow here so a little hare's ear is sent out, an awkward cast. It lands upstream of the rise and is carried down over the trout's position, no response. Again the fly is sent to tempt the trout, again no response. The fish has stopped rising now. The casting and retrieves may have put him down or perhaps spooked a fish which, in turn, signalled to our fish to be watchful.

It is worth trying a nymph; it will sometimes tempt a fish that will not rise. The Option Two is unhitched from the lapel and tied on. A sideways cast places the nymph, with a tiny plop, into the mainstream. The rod is raised and line drawn back to remain in contact, but the line comes back in the current without the tell-tale lift in the bow that signals a fish.

Again, the nymph searches the run, each time any weed is cleared from the hook. Trout do not want vegetables with their meat. The rod is drawn back in readiness for a roll cast forward and the line tightens. A fish. Something briefly grabbed the nymph as it was drawn back. A roll-cast flips the nymph forward and, after a brief pause, the nymph is drawn back, lifting in the water as before. Again that tweak, a flash of silver, and the mystery is resolved; a grayling, just a small one this time, quickly returned.

Leaving the grayling pool there is a lovely little run just around the corner. The river here is tight, a note for the diary read, 'a seven-foot rod is long enough', anything over seven and a half feet makes for frustrating fishing due to the overgrown banks and narrow tunnel of clear space in which to cast. The best stance is to wedge up against the nearside bank so a right hander can swing the little rod sideways over the stream.

In these small border streams, even if wading disturbs the trout, if the angler stands for a while and waits it is surprising how soon a fish will rise again. They begin furthest away and then move closer, until eventually there can be rises under the rod tip. Trout and grayling do this in other pools on the Clun too. I think the pool has to be deep to give them confidence and the angler needs to be standing still in deep water, heavy vegetation no doubt helps, he then becomes part of the river.

A fish is rising just a few rod lengths ahead. Take off the nymph and tie on a Little Hereford size sixteen. A short cast, watching out for the branches behind, and the fly drops just ahead of the spreading rings. Another rise, tight against the bank this time and closer, it pays to tackle the nearest trout first to avoid casting over a fish which will dart upstream and alert his neighbours. This fish is closer, line is reeled in then the side-cast held at the last moment to attempt to flick the fly around into a curve to land the fly over the fish with the line to one side; sounds good in theory, sometimes works in practice. This time the first attempt ends in the branches behind, the second falls in a heap without reaching the fish, the third is reasonable and the fly drifts down just out from the bank. A dark shape that turns into a trout rises up and takes the fly. It is difficult to resist striking too early when the trout can be seen. This time, after a slight pause, the rod is lifted. The trout dives to get back to the roots

The Clun River

under the bank. Now the rod is held hard over and the line cuts through the clear water, pointing to the trout struggling down in the shadows. There is that moment when the full strain from the arched rod is balanced by the power of the wild fish; of course this is no shark or marlin, this is a native small stream trout, a battle of finesse and guile rather than brute force, and the trout, still protesting, is brought to hand.

A tape is useful to record the bigger fish and a shortened dressmaker's tape is brought out. With the trout held by the lower jaw, a position where most trout will lie still for a moment, the tape is quickly laid alongside, twelve inches, the largest so far. He is lowered back to his element and, with a twist, is gone.

The next lie is the head of the pool where the stream runs over shallows before forming a deep run under the nearside bank. The Little Hereford is dried and preened ready to be sent out again. Already a fish can be seen rising in the shallows, but it is likely to be either a pink or parr, better to wait and see if the deeper run reveals a fish. Yes, just tight into the bank, there is a rise. Once more a difficult cast, back into the bank, but a little additional space means there is an angle to cast slightly across stream. The first cast lands in the area but soon drags, an adjustment is made, more slack and hold back slightly as the fly reaches out over the lie. It drops onto the fast run and disappears with a blip, no time to drag. This trout was waiting for food coming down in the fast current and took his chance. Now he must be kept away from the roots that trail in the stream. Once again the rod is brought right over so the side-strain draws him away from his bolt hole. The light rod bends into its fighting curve. It is these first few seconds when a trout can gain refuge, diving into cover, usually into the alder roots that line most border rivers. Once out in the open, unless he is a monster, we should have the beating of him.

He tumbles back down the stream towards the rod; line is stripped back quickly by hand to maintain contact, so now the trout is swimming around directly under the rod tip. Luckily the line is connected to the leader with a glued knotless splice which slips easily though the top ring and saves the embarrassment of twelve feet of leader and tippet, and only six and a half feet of rod.

This trout is well-bred enough to resist the temptation to dive between waders, a trick some trout find hilarious. He is brought to the surface and, once his head is up, he can be skimmed along the surface. He is also worthy of the tape and is recorded in the pocket book at a good twelve inches.

Now is the time to decide where to try next. Border streams may seem small, and the fisheries are sometimes only a field or two in length, but because the streams are small they have more features. There are many more nooks and crannies, twists and turns, and places for a trout to hide than the same length on the main river. They frequently hold many more trout to the mile.

With so many pools to fish, and even a June evening only lasting for so long, it is time to plan where to fish next. Although every pool holds fish, tonight it is best to head for a nice corner pool which is deep and calm, an ideal place to watch for an evening fall of spinners.

The tail of the pool shallows to a gravel beach, now we must slide down the bank into the thin broken water to approach where the trout lie. A careful wade across gives casting room for a right-handed angler to work. Wading slowly, watching for any tell-tale swirls where trout holding in the shallows have darted upstream. Tight against the bank there is only just room for a side-cast. To cast overhead is impossible with the overhanging trees. It is slow work moving up into casting range of the deep heart of the pool.

A couple of fish have already shown their presence by rising, but they were out of range. Closer now, there is a rise near to the far bank. The Little Hereford is once more flicked out across the stream, where it floats down unhindered. A half-roll cast lifts the line. Another rise a little further up shows another fish feeding. The line shoots out and the long leader lays the fly just ahead of the rise. A rise, the trout takes, the rod goes up and in turn the trout is taken. It is just a small fish, nine inches, but another one for the pocket book.

Time now to move carefully forward, sliding into the centre of the pool. With low water and little flow caution is needed and wading tight to the bank reduces disturbance. Where the main flow enters the pool, a line of foam and debris marks out the feeding line. It sweeps across to a labyrinth of alder roots on our side; close by the trout are rising.

On a warm evening after a hot day it is an odds-on bet that there will be spinners on the water and an evening rise. Anglers on chalk-streams bemoan the scarcity of fly life and the lack of an evening rise. Border streams continue to provide good numbers of flies, and frequent evening rises; the difference being a hatch is usually a mixture of flies. Chalk-stream hatches traditionally were single species whereas, on a border stream, insects often don't come with a brand name.

Now, there are spinners dancing over the water, although in the low light it is difficult to see if they are responsible for the rises. Bending low to scan the water's surface the spinners can be seen, some lying spent and some with one wing held aloft.

Perhaps for no better reason than it is nice to fish the spinner, the now waterlogged Little Hereford is taken off and a little Red Spinner is tied on. A smear of floatant, red Mucilin, is worked into the wings and tail with warm fingers so only the slightest film covers the fibres. To degrease the nylon tippet a little moss is picked off the alder roots and run up the line to the fly.

Now the size sixteen pheasant tail spinner hangs ready, its rich deep chestnut red body, (marron, in French) matches the red evening light of the setting sun.

Another rise, and a slow rolling cast strokes the fly out to alight just to the side of the main flow. Here the pool is calm, the spinner lays flat, just a dimple on the surface; then in a swirl, is gone. The rod is raised, and the line stripped back to keep contact. A good fish by the throb, throb, pull on the line. The rod is held down low over the water, not only to avoid the alders, but also to discourage the fish from leaping and splashing about on the surface. Luckily this fellow does not kite off into the roots but instead comes protesting back down the pool until near the rod he stubbornly refuses to come any closer. Here the little rod shows its shortcomings when playing a fish, but he is soon brought under control and entered into the notebook as ten inches.

Time to take stock and check line and fly. When fishing a spent-winged fly it pays to check that the tippet is not being twisted; this time all is well. Sometimes hackle-tip wings, although looking convincing, act as a propeller and twirl and twist the tippet; especially fine nylon.

The fly is preened and held ready for another rise. There, further up, near the head of the pool, once more a quiet rise. Edge forward now, one, two, three steps, and a soft cast curls out and the fly floats down like dandelion floss on the edge of the foam. There are times, when you have been on the water for a while, focus comes together in a moment of calm concentration when, without thinking, without forcing or effort, one simply places the fly.

It is getting dark, especially under the alders, but the evening sun glints on the water and the position of the tiny spinner is marked against a fleck of white foam, and is gone. Spreading rings signal the rise. The rod goes up and the calm is broken. Before a tight line can hold him, this fish leaps against the shock of the hook, and leaps again, twisting in the air, throwing sparkles of water, before splashing back down. When this happens, textbooks tell you to drop the rod tip to avoid being broken, but sometimes you can only stand in wonder. Luckily he is well hooked and comes to hand quietly after his efforts. At twelve inches a good fish, but really can inches ever measure that trout, that moment?

It would be tempting to finish now. 'The shades of night were falling fast', but there is one last pool, the corner pool, that is open and catches the last light of day.

A quick walk upstream now and a slide down the bank into the shallows below the tail of the pool. Good, there are fish rising, but the little spinner will not do. Already bedraggled and waterlogged, it is taken off and by holding the line up to the last light, a Red Sedge is tied on.

In the dusky light the trout are less wary, and now there are rises all over the pool. With less light and time running out a position is quickly

The Clun River

taken at the tail of the pool. As one of the few open areas; it is ideal for fishing into twilight.

The well-greased sedge is flicked out into the main flow. It floats down through the shadows of the far bank following the outside edge of the bend. A rise, and missed, but it is not even clear that the rise was to the artificial. The ever-growing darkness means it is difficult to pick out the fly on the water. The fly is checked and sent back out. There are rises all around now, most are small fish dimpling the surface. A swirl and the rod bends as it makes contact with something alive, struggling out in the darkness. Steady pressure brings the trout closer and soon he is splashing in the shallows. A nice fish, say ten inches, he's slipped off the hook and away.

Nightfall is traditionally the time when the largest and wariest old trout are supposed to venture out to feed. Surely that tangle of roots hides a leviathan in their watery caverns. Unfortunately, thus far, the diary holds no monsters taken at the dying of the day, but there is always hope.

Fish are still rising all over. The fly is rubbed on a tissue and re-greased. Again the sedge goes out to seek that fabled giant, this time it comes back with no response. There are fewer rises now; bats fly low over the river, skimming the pool. This is nearly the end. Another cast, the rod jolts as a bat hits the line. Once the bats appear time is running out, soon the trout will stop rising.

In the darkness, a rise. The rod is lifted at the sound, again the feeling of contact. This time a good Clun trout of ten inches is brought to hand and released. Another nice fish, but not the monster, that will have to wait for another time, another story.

Time to stop; it is difficult sometimes while there are fish still rising, but now there are few rises and it is impossible to see the fly on the water. Some go on fishing into the darkness but much of the pleasure has gone. Unable to see the moment of the rise, or the beauty of the fish it seems to reduce the exercise to simply one of numbers, trout are too important for that.

This is a magic time, standing in the river as sedge flies, moths, bats and faeries flit through the twilight. Now the angler hears the night voice of the river. It is difficult to leave, the moon is up behind the castle, nothing moves now, the rises have finished. The angler's moon shadow will kill the fishing, even if he cannot see it himself. He is surrounded by things of the night; they will not exist when daylight comes.

A white shape moves silently behind the empty windows of the castle, as the angler walks back to the car, and floats down across the meadow to hunt over the long grass.

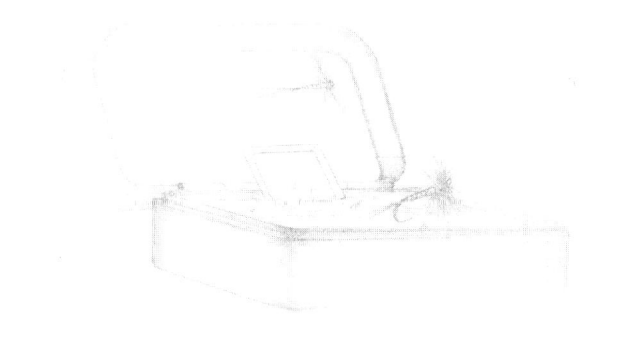

AN EVENING RISE ON THE REA

Seasons on the River Rea could be classed as, early spring when flies and fish are scarce, late spring when fly life is more plentiful and fish rise throughout the day, mayfly time when monsters may rise, and finally high summer when all is hot and dry and the river seems to be drowsing. Then only movement is the odd rise in the shadow of the alders, but wait until evening, once the heat of the day has left the water, flies will hatch and trout will rise. High summer is a good time to fish in the evenings after work.

Here is one such evening in July after the main mayfly hatch. It has been a blazing hot day, the valley swelters on the hottest day of the year so far. Everyone who has been waiting for summer now says, 'it's too hot'. Conditions are perfect for an evening rise.

The day has been spent in a hot office, glazed eyes staring at the screen, on such days as these it is bliss to go down to the river. The church clock shows half past seven as we motor through

Cleobury Mortimer and round the crooked spire. The sound of bells, it is Wednesday, practice night. Not much further now to the farm.

The valley of the little River Rea opens out as the car rolls down the farm track to the river. The sun is golden in a cloudless blue sky and a faint smell of dust hangs in the still, warm air. A small group of spinners dance over the car roof; it is an evening for a cane rod and a small dry fly. Tonight it is an outing for 'the old rod', an ancient eight-foot by Hardy. To match it, a Hardy lightweight reel. A four-weight line is threaded through the rings and we are ready to go.

This evening trout are rising all along the little river. It will be nice to work upstream to fish the 'New Water'. So called because it was added to the fishery after I took up the fishing here. Now even the 'New Water' has been part of the fishery for more than twenty years.

It starts halfway up with a rocky pool misleadingly named 'Top pool'. It was the top pool of the fishery until the New Water was added. A steep drop down the short sheep cropped grass leads to the slabs of rock that form the tail of the pool.

Today it is an ideal place to start, the alders over-hang and provide shade while upstream there is a long, broken riffle. It is a good spot, and already a rise, at the tail of the pool, possibly a small fish but worth a try.

As the water is quite fast and broken, a general pattern should suffice. First delve into the jacket pocket for some tippet material, there are two small spools of nylon, fine and finer. Start with two-and-a-half-pound breaking-strain first, keep the two pound in reserve. A size sixteen Adams is tied on. Lengthen the line and drop the fly on the water just where the rise was seen. He rises further over. Another cast places the fly directly in front and just a little ahead. Perfect, apart from the drag, the faster water at the tail catches the line and drags the fly, trailing it across the rocks and twigs in the tail of the pool. Time to bring in the fly, clean and dry it, and wait to see if the trout was put down by the blunder.

An Evening Rise on the Rea

He rises again. Step across the stream and get directly below him. Less angle, less line across the current. Fly-fishing, like snooker, is about angles. This time the fly drops lightly in the target zone, a splash and he is on. Not the most confident rise, perhaps he was spooked, but he's on and, despite a brave struggle, he is brought tumbling into the shallow water and quickly unhooked. Just a second to take in the bright yellow flanks, spotted red and black, and white stripe on pectoral leading edge. He twists and is away. A moment now to jot down, '10" #16 Adams Top Pool' and add '18° calm/bright sun 7.45pm start'. It is enough to jog the memory when the diary is filled in before bedtime.

Attention is now focused on the head of the pool, hopefully not disturbed. The main flow is marked by a foam line, debris and flies brought down over the waiting trout. A splash, was it a rise? Just a disturbance in the broken water, but to an angler it is a chance of a fish. There, again a rise, definitely. Now is the time to get in position for the cast, crouched low to avoid the overhanging alders. The little Adams drops in the swirling water and a blink and the fly has gone. Lift the rod and now something strong and full of life is struggling deep in the pool. The rod goes up to keep his head out of the rocks, a yellow flash as he twists and fights against the pull. There is magic somewhere, in the waving of a wand over the dark face of the water, to conjure up this bright jewel full of life. He comes to hand, a little bigger this time, the note reads '11"Adams #16 Top pool'.

It is time to move on. Next, a long run, the first in the New Water, called 'Heavens Run'. Here it's necessary to wade up a long tunnel of overhanging alders. Tuck in and side cast, fine if you are right-handed. There is a feeding lane down the deeper channel under the trees.

Now a moment to stop and stare, and there, tight in the channel, a good rise. It is an unavoidable choice, to wade through the shallows and risk spooking a fish, thus disturbing the rest of the pool, or wait and lose time and possibly the chance of a rising fish. Count to twenty, slowly, and with no rises close in, and another rise ahead the choice is made.

An Evening Rise on the Rea

The evening rise is short, time to move carefully into position, one step, another, creeping slow to avoid a bow wave pushing up ahead. There, another rise, unclip the Adams and a slow side swipe from the cane rod rolls the line out to drop the fly on the feeding line. It travels down without incident. Another cast, again in line but a little further ahead, give him chance to see it, nothing, and then a rise, a confident rise to a natural where the fly had covered.

No sense in trying again, bring in the Adams and have a think. The fly that worked on the quick broken water did not work on the calmer water of Heavens Run. It could be that a lower riding fly such as an F Fly, or Duck's Dun might work, but that rise looked different, a sort of swirl, a deep bulging, rather than a splashy surface rise, maybe this fish is taking something in, or just under, the surface.

At this time in the season the blue-winged olive often hatches on the Rea, usually in the evenings. Here it is quite a small fly, a small sixteen, in fly-dressers terms. Notoriously difficult to imitate according to chalk-stream anglers, the trout often take it as it emerges. A good pattern in this situation is a Neen Nymph, one is tied on, spit on its tail and lightly grease the hare's ear. This collar is teased out sufficiently to keep it afloat while the soaked tail hangs below the surface to tempt the trout.

The trout is still rising. It looks like the bulge of a heavy fish. Some say on chalk-streams that the heaviest fish make the smallest rises; not on these border streams, it is usually bigger fish that move the most water, a heave and wave rather than a little splash, is usually the sign of a good fish.

The cast drops the little nymph in line with the last rise; chances are he will not move far off line if he is feeding close to the surface. A confident bulge signals the take and a lift of the rod tightens into a heavy fish that plunges upstream. The old cane rod bends to a battle curve, transmitting the force through to the hand. He's a very good fish, fighting the strain from the line, the rod softens the ferocity of the fight but still the fine nylon tippet is strained to its limit. If he should get into those tree roots now it would be over. Constant side strain, the trout is fighting the rod, the drag of the line, and the current, but still he's deep, not broken surface. Move to the side, get a better position to lead him away from the roots, and take the opportunity to wind in loose line. Now he's boring deep and dropping down, keep the line tight, keep the strain on, he'll use any let up in pressure to reach those roots. Now he's opposite and there is a gleam deep down as he turns. He's tiring but this is a dangerous time, to his weight is now added the force of the current. Walk him downstream and keep opposite, don't let him get below, if he goes over the sill at the tail of the pool he could still be lost. Now he is lying in the current, tired, he needs to be unhooked and set free. He's brought closer, a last strong run, and then his head comes up to break surface. Now he's beat. Pinch his jaw to get a firm grip and run the tape down his flank, the Neen Nymph is just caught in his jaw and falls away at the touch. He is laid in the water and cradled, head up-stream, just chance to admire the bulk of him across the matt olive brown shoulders, sixteen inches, one of the biggest this year, and one of the best. Feel that strength returning now as his gills pump water. He's just lying there, not sure he's free, a movement of the hand and he's away, back down in his pool below the alder roots. Once more the notebook, '16″ Neen Nymph #16 Heavens Run'.

The upper stretch of Heavens Run often produces fish; indeed it is possible to work upstream taking fish all along. This time there is one fish rising regularly under an overhanging alder. It is a bit tight.

The reason the run is full of fish is the overhanging branches, but that is of little use if it is impossible to fish, a balance must be struck. Overhanging branches on the fishery are trimmed to about three feet, or a metre above the stream, it seems about right.

Crouching in the water, inches from the surface, it seems very tight, very intimate. Luckily, it is only a short cast, the fish is just a couple of rod lengths ahead. He is rising regularly; it is just possible to see the dark shadow coming to the surface. A side cast is needed, careful not to fire it into the water, luckily the line flicks around and the little Neen Nymph lands lightly in place. A confident rise and he's on. Quickly the rod goes over and side strain hauls him away from the roots, he runs upstream and leaps, and leaps again. Spectacular in the evening sunshine, an image that remains. Now tiring he is quickly brought to hand and unhooked, a quick estimate, twelve inches, a nice fish.

Above Heavens Run is a shallow stretch that sometimes produces a fish, but tonight it is bypassed as time is tight and the next big pool beckons. Paradise Pool is above Heavens Run, naturally. A large deep pool of slow water, what an American angler once called a PhD pool, because the trout there, well, you get the idea.

Squat low at the tail. Trout hold in the shallows and usually more than one fish. The Neen Nymph is unclipped from the keeper ring and rubbed in the mud of the waterside. Drag will be a problem here. Trout will take a sunken nymph speeding up and away but they are often spooked by a dragging surface fly. As ever, it is a case of watching the water for rises. There are at least two trout rising in the main pool.

Then, just as the line is readied for a long cast, a rise close in. Drop lower now and shorten the line, just a short flick, held back to land with a slack tippet. The nymph sinks, but the current over the sill quickly picks up the line and pulls it away. Another cast and rod held high gives a few more seconds in the zone. No response, maybe disturbed he has moved into deeper water, no, another rise. This time the nymph drops spot on, and there is a bulge as it is taken. A smaller fish this, bundled over the sill into the fast water below, he is held and unhooked before he really knows what is going on. Hopefully the pool remains undisturbed.

Now to move into position to cover the main body of the pool. Then there's another rise in the tail, this time to the side. A cast is sent in his direction, or it would have if the back cast hadn't gone into the tall grass behind and then, once freed, a clumsy cast drops the nymph bang on his head. As the old river keepers would say, 'I think he might have seen that one, sir'. That's small river fishing. Take a deep breath. Mr Crabtree would have lit up a pipe, a chocolate bar will do.

Settle down and watch the pool. While crouched down on the sill of the pool it is clear that, amongst the hatching olives, there are some flies lying spent on the surface. By now the sun has sunk

An Evening Rise on the Rea

below the surrounding hills and the trout rise confidently in the dusk. One is rising towards the head of the pool, then another rises closer in. The rises are dimples rather than a heave or swirl, the closest one is rising frequently, he will be first.

A little red spinner, lightly dressed on a size sixteen fine wire hook, is tied on to mimic the spent fly. Three feet of fine nylon is added to the cast to replace the tippet shortened by retying flies. The generous length and fine nylon will help the fly drift more naturally.

Shuffling back quietly into place, back into the rhythm, a cast is placed gently across the pool to land just ahead of the last rise. Fishing a tiny spent fly, on fine line is surely the distillation of dry fly delicacy. This time the fly is ignored, it drifts past. There is another rise, slightly to the side. The old rod lifts the line off the water; the slow rhythm of the split-cane lays the line on the surface like a brush stroke. Trying to think the fly into position.

For a moment nothing exists but the water, the fly, and the rise. Fishing is about focus, nothing casual only concentration, and a belief that a fish will rise. When the trout takes the fly, the rod lifts and connection with the real world returns. A nice fish, held hard in the tail of the pool but fighting against the rod. The cane, golden in the evening light, bent into its fighting curve becomes alive, tip jabbing to point out where the trout is hidden deep in the pool. He tires and is brought in, head up, to be unhooked and then he pushes back strongly for the depths.

Although it is mid-summer, the light is failing. It is past ten o' clock and already the first few bats are about. The evening is always planned to end on an open pool. Runs under trees are in deep shadow now, only the open water is fishable. A torch would extend the time available to tie on a fresh fly, but then when would you ever go home?

There is just enough time to approach one more fish, to an angler there is always one more fish, one more cast. Less need for crouching now, approach closer, check the fly and cast into the darkness. The fly lands softly, but is not taken. He is still rising, twice the rod is lifted in anticipation, but the rise was to a natural fly. Will the evening end with a fish? Yes, he's on. By sound and feel the line is tightened onto the fish, the rise heard more than seen. Hold hard and trust in your tackle. Backing out now, into clearer water, the curve of the rod is seen against the last glow in the western sky. Bend down and hold the fish for a moment, a nice fish, twelve inches, maybe more. He swims off a dark shape in the water.

The angling evening is over; the gold of sunset has turned into the silver of the night. Somewhere a dog barks and from a farm across the valley, another answers. All that remains is the walk back along the river as darkness falls, stumbling over rough banks to find the familiar crossing place. Then aim towards the farm house lights, and the car, a last mouthful of coffee before the drive home in the dark, with a smile.

AN EVENING ON THE TEME

A warm summer's evening during the mayfly season is probably one of the best times to fish the Teme. The mayfly is fairly punctual in its appearance and the first show up on the Teme around the middle of May, but they can be delayed a week or so by a cold spring. Watch for them when the sand martins return to swoop and wheel around the Teme bridge in Tenbury. Good hatches occur through June and even in July a few can still be seen.

The water, on this day from the diary, is Bednals, a favourite stretch; it is a good level and running clear. Easy walking distance from Tenbury town centre, a track from the Berrington road brings the angler to the river.

Typically for the Teme the path is high above the river. The first entry point is down an old iron ladder to what was a good salmon pool, called the 'Bell Hole', sadly no salmon have been recorded from its depths for decades.

An Evening on the Teme

Just upstream are the 'Bednal Flats', shallow steps of sandstone that sometimes hold a small trout in deeper holes and crevices when there is sufficient water.

A pause, and wait. It is a moment to watch the river, to adjust to the pace of the water, and most importantly notice things, the sand martins sweeping over the river feeding on flies or the rise of a trout. Trout will give themselves away with a rise, but nothing, nothing moves, except a few mayflies dancing in the evening sunlight. In the distance a sulphur-coloured Yellow May Dun is highlighted against the dark alders, taking to the air near the confluence of the little Bednal brook.

When fishing in the evening, time is always in short supply, so now move on back up the ladder and further down the river. A short distance further there is a track, hidden in the summer vegetation. A scramble down the bank drops the angler onto the water at the tail of the Bell Hole, a wide gliding shallow that holds grayling in the autumn. A pied wagtail, the 'water wagtail' bobs on a rock and flies off as a careful approach is made.

Crouching low and scanning the water there is a confident rise midstream. A spent mayfly pattern is ready and the line stripped out to cover the fish. Hold, a fish rises close in, and just a little upstream. A minute later and the midstream cast would have 'lined' him. Reel in and shorten the line. There again the rise, a little further upstream and tight into the nearside bank. The cast goes out, the large mayfly drops awkwardly on one side, and floats down untouched. Picked up with a roll cast and the line lengthened, another cast places the fly nearer to the correct line, but still no response. A rise, the same fish, another cast, the same result.

Meanwhile the midstream fish is rising confidently. Time to change focus. Shuffling across to a sandstone bar midstream gives a better angle to cover him. So the line is adjusted to cover this new fish – when the first fish rises again.

This time the angle of the light and the shadow of an alder allow the fish to be seen. Still tight against the bank he looks large, very large. A grey shape against the bottom he hardly moves. One more cast, line is shortened, and this time from a better position the fly lands perfectly, directly in front of his nose. Slowly he rises, he's huge, but as he comes to the surface he gives his identity away, Mr Chub. Big white lips slowly engulf the fly. Sometimes chub are hard to hook, but not this time. A gentle lift and he dives down, his size putting a bend in the rod that a trout would find hard to equal. A moderate chub is equal in size to a very good trout, but not in stamina. The fight is soon over. Although just within season the chub will still be getting over spawning and not at his best. He swings in the current showing his great bronze and brass flank, a moment later the barbless mayfly is slipped from his rubbery lips and he swims back to his lie below the alder tree. No need for the net, although a short-handled net rests in the small of my back, tucked under the wading belt. It is a good idea to have a landing net in these situations, to deal with chub and monster May-time trout.

So far, on this perfect trout fishing evening, the total result has been one moderately sized chub. If this were Mr Crabtree, by now Peter would have had a brace and Mr Crabtree would be fast into a two pounder. However, this is real life and this is the way it happened. At least there is a fish to record. This evening won't be fishless, 'water whacked' we called it as kids. The midstream fish is still rising. He is easy to mark because he is rising at the point where the alder branches reach out over the water. The mayfly is dried, lightly greased and preened into shape before being sent out.

Casting mayflies on long leaders and fine tippets is likely to end with a tangle, even on a fairly strong and stiff leader they are difficult. Luckily this one lands as intended and, after a short drift, comes an emphatic take. Lift the rod, no snatching with the mayfly, it pays to allow the fish to turn down with the fly. Tradition would have the angler say 'God save the Queen' first. A lively tugging at the other end signals the trout is hooked. The rod bends to the determined fight of the fish and is angled over to draw the fish to the side, to avoid disturbing the main body of the pool. He is defiant to the last, but no monster, he has to submit to the strain of the rod. Held by his bottom jaw the fly is revealed in the top of his mouth and removed by forceps. A shake of his head and he swims quickly away to grow bigger and wiser. Pause to add another note

An Evening on the Teme

alongside the chub in the pocket notebook. 'Trout, nine inches, Bell Hole Run, M/F spent.'

A fish, no matter his size, should have the tribute of being recorded for his efforts. The pause serves another purpose too, another fish rises. This fish is further across and upstream. Line is pulled from the reel, and a cast rolls out across the river. The fish rises again, a little further out, another pull of line and a bit more effort. The line lands in a heap, well, perhaps not a heap, but far short of its target. Smile, it's better than cursing. After thirty years still not learnt that the fly line can't be forced –it's like pushing water uphill.

Carefully wade forward to a reasonable range, and the next cast lands on target, but is ignored. Sidle forward a few more steps, again the fly lands just ahead of his marked position and hasn't travelled far when it disappears in a good rise. The rod is raised and contact made, this time there is no stopping his first rushes. A good fish on a long line he scythes across the pool. For a moment the fly line is drawn from the dark water and spray sparkles in the evening sunlight as the trout leaps, a curve of yellow vigour. He struggles to break free but the pool is clear of snags and he is eventually brought to hand still protesting. The white bodied mayfly spinner is clear to see caught in the corner of his jaw. Hold the hook shank and rotate it out, the barbless hook comes free and he swims uncertainly away. At a good twelve inches another for the notebook.

Live creatures shouldn't be reduced to numbers but there is something satisfying about 'a brace'. Now, whatever happens, the evening's fishing is a success. To go fishing and catch a fish, is a fundamental sense of achievement. It takes a few years to get past the fundamental sense of frustration stage when achievement is rare and trout few and far between. A kingfisher arrows down the river, jinking aside to avoid the angler standing in the stream.

The evening is still young, while this run may not yield another rising trout, the rest of Bednals is ready to be explored. Onwards, downstream take a look at the deep cleft in the sandstone where the river runs slow and cavernous through a divide in the rocks. Despite the mayfly hatch nothing rises, although it always looks as if it could harbour a leviathan.

A little further the river forms a pool, just upstream of the confluence of the Ledwyche, if you wish to fish it yourself. This pool again is reputed to have held salmon, and its deep dark waters look the part. It is a slow rotating eddy with the main flow along the far bank.

In the summer a shoal of chub lie under the far bank alders and their rises lure trout anglers as surely as sirens lure sailors. Towards the tail in the faster water there is a rise, the solid energetic rise of a trout, rather than the gentle sip of a chub. The back cast here is restricted by the steep bank, and after a trip into the bushes to retrieve the fly, the spent mayfly is cast over the trout's position, another rises further up. Once again the mayfly is sent out, again no response.

These trout cruising in the slower water of the pool have no need to rush, they pick the spinners circling in the flow and the tethered artificial is soon detected. The text book will say to throw a line with a lot of slack, and will even name the casts for you, which seems good in theory but, if you watch the line and tippet carefully, the fly usually drags before the line has had chance to straighten out.

Another solution is needed. Watching the water carefully, although there are spinners about, the rises are not to anything obvious, maybe the trout are taking the emerging mayfly.

An unweighted nymph pattern is tied on. If this drags slightly it still may be taken, indeed a slight lift often brings a result. Not this time, a tweak as a curious trout nips at it, then nothing.

There are still mayfly hatching so the nymph is taken off and a low riding mayfly is tied on. It is a sombre green in colour with the lower hackle cut away, hopefully it looks like an emerging mayfly dun. Some anglers may pass these awkward fish by, while others cannot resist the challenge to convert every rise into a fish, or at least a fish hooked or risen, a determination to deceive each and every trout.

Wait for a rise, he rises again, the fly is readied and sent out to land lightly just in front of his position. The mayfly sits low on the water, wings cocked, looking very like a newly emerged mayfly climbing out of its shuck. It disappears, replaced by the rings of a rise. The rod is raised and finds an answer from the trout who dives for the depths. The water here is quite clear of snags so it is fairly easy to hold him in the pool giving a little side strain to throw him off balance and soon, despite his game struggles, he is brought back to the bank where the large barbless hook is easy to grasp and release.

It is with some satisfaction that this hard-won trout is entered into the note book '10" low riding M/F dun', then a pause, this pool has a name but it can't be brought to mind. With some feeling it is entered as 'Desperation Deep'.

Time to move on to what is probably the best run of the Bednals section, the Garden Pool. So called because it runs the length of the garden of the big house whose mown lawns run down the far bank. In summertime visitors explore the big house and stroll around the gardens, some stand on the close mown lawns and gaze over the river. How different now, the visitors have all gone home, or to the pub, and the river is left to nature, and the angler.

Flyfishers approach the pool, wading up from the shallow tail with the river flowing down under their right arm. The path to get there is through a nettle bed, it is best approached with arms raised as the nettles are up to chin height. As there is no path beaten through it seems no one has fished here in a while. The nettles stop atop a short steep bank leading down to a shingle beach, just then a pair of mallard take off, noisily, from the tail of the pool and go quacking upstream.

Time to stand and watch a while, and suck a sweet while the pool calms down. Eventually there is a good rise, across by the far bank. Now, a cautious approach is needed, edging across the shallow water at the tail of the pool to get below the rise and avoid those arrowing marks that show a trout has been alarmed and means to spread panic through the rest of the pool.

All is well and a comfortable and steady stance is found on the pebbly bed. Draw line from the reel now and try a cast, it goes out short, lengthen line and send it out again. It is the same Mayfly Dun imitation that worked on the previous pool, and again it sits nicely cocked and rides back down the stream. Another rise a little further up. To avoid stretching it is necessary to mark the rise against the trailing grass on the bank and edge closer. The lie of the trout is comfortably in range now, pause, check that he hasn't been put down by any clumsy wading, no, there is another rise.

A careful cast, with a slight check at the end, sends the Mayfly to drop lightly just in front of his nose. A rise, contact is made, once more the trout is steered away from the main flow, he objects by jumping, bouncing into the air in a series leaps. It is impossible not to smile at the sight of a golden yellow trout leaping in the evening light. Hopefully he hasn't alerted the whole pool. As sometimes happens, the leaps have taken the fight out of him and he allows himself to be bundled downstream and pressure brings his head up. He is slid to hand and quickly released. Time to fill in the note book '10" low rider M/F dun Garden Pool', and unwrap another sweet, a fruit drop goes well with the summer weather, leaving the mint humbugs for the autumn grayling.

The fruit drop does its work and a trout rises upstream, just below an overhanging willow bush.

It is too far to reach from this position. A careful move is required, trying not to make waves as waders push against the current in the calm pool. A pause and the trout rises again, no two, a second rise a couple of seconds later shows that there are two trout. One is tucked right under the trailing willow while the other is a little further out into the main stream.

They are within range now and a preliminary cast lands the fly short and to one side, an adjustment, and another cast, with a slight check to flick out the big Mayfly and turn over the leader. It lands lightly and floats over the trout's position. The fly disappears into the rings of a rise. The rod goes up and is immediately hooped over as a large trout heads off upstream. Sweep the rod over to the side now applying strain to keep him away from the trailing willow, he powers on, creating a bow wave as his tail propels him forward. This is a good fish, the rod is bowed over bending to the power of the fish. His run has taken him midstream and the rod can be held low to discourage him from leaping. He is fighting the rod and the current, however big he is he cannot resist, nor does he for the line slackens as he runs downstream heading for the far bank. Line is stripped back in by hand and contact maintained, now he is slightly downstream and he has the advantage of the current, luckily the pool is calm and the current slight, he twists and kicks trying to make the far bank roots but he is tiring and the rod absorbs his struggles until he can be rolled over and brought to the net. He lies in the flow and the net is readied. Medium sized trout can be unhooked without the use of a net, to avoid damage and stress. Larger trout tend to object to this rather casual treatment by twisting and kicking which shreds the angler's thumb and more importantly may damage the fish, a small net is best. He is quickly scooped up.

With the rod tucked under arm, crouch to follow the line to the fly. The big Mayfly is obvious and easily removed. The tape now, the trout lies still in the water cradled by the net. A splendid fish beautifully marked with large spots and a really solid specimen, broad across the shoulders sixteen or fifteen inches? The note book records '15" good cond. Low rider M/F dun, Garden Pool'.

Time to sort out tackle, tidy away the net, dry and preen the fly, and another fruit drop. The sun has sunk below the trees now, there is a hush in the valley as the evening draws in. Another rise, where there were two trout rising, the remaining fish is still feeding. He rises tight into the trailing willow bush, taking flies that are swept between the hanging branches, an almost impossible position.

A slow and careful approach brings him within easy casting range, any cast will need to be precise and this is close up work. He rises again and his dark shape can be seen for a second just below the surface as he takes a mayfly spinner that floats down one wing up, the other spent.

A cast goes out, short, it will do no harm, another lands just short of the trailing leaves, did he look at it? No rise and the fly comes back in the current. He is rising frequently now but to show him the same Mayfly pattern may put him down. The dun is a little tatty and waterlogged, time to try something different, a spent pattern looks a good match for those he has taken. It is tied on along with a new length of tippet.

An Evening on the Teme

The first cast lands just as he rises to a natural, it is ignored but line and length are now established and the next drops the fly between two trailing branches, and it is gone, replaced by the rings of a rise. The rod lifts into him and the water explodes into a froth, hold him away from the willow roots at all costs, before he has chance to gain his balance he is hustled out of danger and into clearer water. He still fights on the surface and, being on a tight line, takes his chance to leap, twisting against the taut line. The rod is dropped now the low angle deters him from leaping and he fights deep. For the first time in the fight the angler has control and loose line can be reeled in. He kites across to the nearside alders, it is difficult to stop him as he uses the tight line to slice across the current, he must be stopped and the rod is looped over, putting on pressure to strain the tackle to its limit. He is off balance and spins and kicks, the rod jags as this wild trout twists and then runs downstream, pulling the line in a long curve around the angler. For a moment it is difficult to know just where he is, then contact is regained. Walk down to him now, keeping him on a tight line, he has fired his best shots, now he can be held, he plunges, twisting, stubborn to the last. The net is lowered into the water, he is held hard now until at last his head comes up and he can be brought over the rim. He looks the twin of the previous, 16"? No, just shy, '15" spent M/F Garden Pool' is recorded in the note book. He goes back to find his companion under the willow bush.

Why two similarly sized large fish? It is difficult to say, of course the natural wild trout are numerous around 10" and there was nothing to say these fish were anything but wild. No stocking had taken place that year for several miles upstream or down so they were unlikely to be newly stocked. They may have been stocked at the beginning of the previous season and lived wild and overwintered in the river, who knows?

It has been a good evening and that fine brace has rounded off a good catch, three brace-six trout and a bonus chub.

The Teme isn't always an easy river to fish and the novice can be frustrated, but take time to learn a few of her secrets, watch and be prepared to put in some time and you will be rewarded. Try to get to the river at mayfly time and there is sure to be a fish or two ready to take your fly.

AUTUMN

Keats described autumn as the 'season of mists and mellow fruitfulness', to the angler on the Teme it is the season for grayling, for if springtime belonged to the trout, autumn brings the grayling to the fore.

The river runs through orchards and hop fields where the fruit is now ripe on the trees and the bines. Apples, pears, cherries, plums and damsons all grow in profusion in the mild climate, and the hop yards and oasthouses, found along the Teme, give the valley a special flavour. With luck the weather will stay fine and then, on sunny days, the clear air and crystal light of autumn will illuminate each leaf on the riverside trees. Later, after the first frosts, they will show their autumnal colours, the golden yellow of the birch, the fiery reds of the sycamore, each tree adding to the kaleidoscope of colour in the valley. Nature is putting on a final show before chill wintery winds whip the last of the leaves from the branches to send them dancing on to the river,

Autumn

where they float down the stream or wash around in eddies by the bank.

Now the angler puts on his warm jacket. On his walk to the riverbank he will brustle through the leaves lying under the churchyard chestnuts, while underfoot on the riverbank the wet leaves lie plastered on the damp earth. On quiet mornings jewelled threads hang in the corner of the gate and in the hedge beaded webs sparkle.

Autumn frosts replace summer dew. Often clear blue skies will follow a frosty night and early morning mists are burnt away by the warmth of the sun. On such still autumn days the white smoke from a bonfire rises as a slender spire, pointing to the heavens and cock pheasants can be heard calling in the woods. These frosty nights will often clear the water, the river can run clearer on days after a frost. This is the time to meet 'the lady of the stream', the grayling.

The Teme is rightly renowned for its grayling fishing. In 1824 the Shropshire Gazetteer said 'The Teme is celebrated for grayling; there is also trout in plenty', little has changed. At one time the single-track railway which ran up the valley could have carried the angler.

Back then, horse drawn carriages plied the road that rambles down from Mamble and runs beside the Teme. They brought those earlier anglers who roomed at the bow fronted Swan Hotel overlooking the river.

If we are blessed with a Michaelmas summer, and low, clear water in September and October, the grayling will shine amidst the sparkling waters. Then is the time when the pursuit of grayling with a fly will be at its best. The grayling is an ardent riser to the fly, though fly life is less abundant than it was in summer.

In the autumn, on the Teme, fly life is mainly various small olives, pale wateries or spur wings, with a few sedges thrown in. Grayling seem less fussy about the hatch, but will be fickle as to the size of the fly and how it sits on the water, if a small low riding fly is needed a Gold Ribbed Hare's Ear or Little Hereford fits the bill.

If few fish rise, the angler may seek out the shoals that lie in the fast waters of the fords and swift runs with a wet-fly, a little Red Tag or Worcestershire Gem, or tie on a Burford Red and fish it around until contact is made.

Watch for a number of dimpling rises in the midstream which is the sign of a shoal of grayling, trout rise singly and spread themselves along the stream where they normally hug the banks and other cover.

Finding the grayling shoals is paramount, for while it can be difficult to catch grayling if they will not take the fly, if they are not there, it is impossible. Once found, mark the place well.

As the days grow shorter and some of the warmth goes from the sun, flies become scarce and the grayling will no longer rise. Now the angler may turn to trotting with his float tackle. He has now learnt where the shoals lie, so he may send his red tipped float down the runs to seek out his prize. A rise is a wonderful thing when fly-fishing, but to see that red tipped float dip and go under, held by something unknown and unseen, never fails to excite. It is enjoyable to change the fly rod for the long trotting rod. Even fly-fishers, who praise the finesse of their branch of the art, enjoy the delicacy of the small hook, light line, and skilful manipulation of tackle, as the grayling fisher uses his long reaching rod to guide his bait through each run, seeking out fish in stream and eddy, at different levels, now holding the bait back and then letting it swing up to tempt the hidden fish.

If the angler seeks more sport, the chub and the barbel will still take a bait, they will be fit and willing to feed. A day after the bronze chub or, that prince of the river, the barbel makes for a splendid outing; but that is for another time, and another book.

When to stop? it can be difficult to lay down the tackle for the year, anglers are always prone to take 'one last cast' and it is always tempting to fit in one last trip to the river. Such trips are rarely worthwhile except for exercise, and to satisfy the angler that the cup has been drained.

GRAYLING BELOW THE AQUEDUCT

It is early October. The weather is fine and dry; the river is running clear, tempting the angler to reach for the fly rod.

Clear sunny days have been followed by cold nights, but there will still be a few flies hatching and fish rising. Besides, days with the fly rod are running out, soon it will be the turn of the float. The sun has lost its summer warmth, these days are the last dregs of the 'sweet summer wine'. Now is the time to make the most of the season and go in pursuit of grayling with the fly.

Today's location is the fast water below the aqueduct. Here rocky slabs and fast runs over gravel provide a home for grayling in autumn. Later, as winter closes in, they move into deeper water and form tighter shoals. Each grayling caught, perhaps when after trout, can reveal the position of a shoal. After a while the angler will build up a knowledge of the river and the best places to seek 'the lady of the stream'.

A moment now to talk about the aqueduct, those keen to start fishing may hurry on for a page or two. As most anglers have a fondness for bridges, especially those spanning rivers, here is a story.

The aqueduct above Little Hereford is a grand piece of Victorian engineering. It is one of those structures said to contain a million bricks, maybe so, should you wish to count them. It was built to carry a canal over the Teme on its way from Stourport to Kington by way of Leominster back in the days when this was thought to be a good idea. Alas, the project was beset with problems and was never fully completed. Although it did carry coal from the mines around Mamble and Bayton to Leominster in the years following its opening at the end of the 18th century, railways were to take over and this part of the canal was taken over by a railway company. Today the track of the railway line is no more than an overgrown embankment. The rails also took short cuts and bypassed the aqueduct, the site of the railway bridge is further downstream.

Jump ahead to 1941, the story goes that a member of the Home Guard burst into a pub in Tenbury where his comrades were drinking.

"Quick, quick! The Germans have invaded Greete!" He gasped.

In order to delay the onslaught on Ludlow from the German Panzers now in the little village of Greete, the pals dashed out and blew up the nearest crossing point, the aqueduct. Only then did they realise that the Germans had in fact invaded Crete. Good story: not true.

The local Home Guard[2] did help blow up the aqueduct, but as part of an organised operation with, so I was told, friends and wives invited to watch.

The Teme did constitute a Stop Line[3] from Ludlow down to its confluence near Worcester. There were tank obstructions[4] on either end of the Little Hereford bridge with slit trenches on the canal bed on top of the bank overlooking the road and the Little Hereford Village Hall. No one

---

[2] 7 Battalion Shropshire Home Guard
[3] Western Command Stop Line No 28 1940/41
[4] Now hidden by road repairs

should take too lightly the courage of those who, in such dark times, planned to halt the German Army on the banks of the River Teme.

Well, we have been caught in an eddy, now to return to the main flow. The first pool under the broken arch of the aqueduct, usually holds the odd trout and maybe a small shoal of grayling where the current picks up between the rocks at the tail of the pool. In truth, the casting is awkward and not really worth the effort, better to pass it by.

As the river flows on into the next pool it opens out and forms a fast run, with broken water at the head and a broad shallow ford at the tail. This is one of the best places to ford the river, with low summer flow it is possible to cross in wellingtons. In winter it is the site of salmon redds.

The ivy-hung brick arch looms out of the overhanging bankside alders, towering over the river, a relic of a lost civilisation. It is an angling pitch in the picturesque style; something that Capability Brown might have created.

The bank drops steeply down to the river. A path terraced into the slope shows the way through the trees. Brushing past the tough springy twigs of alder and over the margin of balsam brings the angler to where a small gravel beach leads to the water and from which it is possible to wade into a comfortable spot to fish.

Today, with few fish rising, a position is taken at the head of the pool in order to run a wet-fly back down. If flies had been hatching in any number, and grayling rising, dry fly may have been the choice. Then the approach would have been from the tail, working up to cover each rise in turn until the head of the pool was reached. The decision is simply which is the most efficient or effective, or to be honest the mood of the day.

So with rod tucked under one arm, the fly box is opened and a suitable fly must be selected. The water at the head of the pool is fast and broken, maybe a weighted nymph? An Option 2 seems a good choice for the point, heavy enough to get down in the water and anchor the cast; it is sometimes known as a 'stretcher'. As the river here is wide, wading into the midstream gives clear room for casting and using a second fly on a dropper will cause no problems. A March Hare makes a good dropper; despite its name it is useful all year round. A good representation of a hatching olive, it is tied on and wetted with spit so it will sink straight away.

Now the line is stripped from the reel, six long pulls and a loop of line is carried from the rod by the flow. With line out it can be half flicked, half rolled, into the fast current. The tug of the line plucks the nymph from between finger and thumb, and pitches it into the water, here it will swing into the stream. A little line is let out to guide the flies across the fast flow. Each time a little more line is stripped off the reel until a comfortable amount is out. Easy rolling casts drop the team of flies across to the far side of the stream.

Each time a cast is made a step is taken down the stream in order to cover the water. The weighted nymph holds deep while the March Hare flickers across the stream just below the surface. There, a swirl, just as the dropper caught in the current and started to fish across. The spot is noted, try again. Watch carefully as the flies come into the crease of the currents – and he's on.

The long-reaching rod, which nodded to the pull of the current, now hoops over as the grayling plunges into the stream. There is the tug-tug pull characteristic of the grayling, the strong surge of water at the head of the pool boosts his battle against the line. The rod held high cushions the strain on the fine nylon as he seeks sanctuary at the bed of the stream. Angled over to the side the rod pulls him off balance and he can be guided into the slack water at the side of the run where, after a last attempt to dive deep, he is brought to the surface and pulled over the net.

The slender grayling is a fine-looking fish. This one is long but probably weighs just a little over half a pound. The large dorsal fin is square and shorter than that of the male grayling, (his reaches back to the adipose fin when laid flat,) showing her to be female. The barbless March Hare is slipped out.

Take a moment to appreciate the beauty of the fish cradled in the net. She is known as the 'lady of the stream' because of her graceful and lithe lines, but don't be fooled, she is strong and assertive often bullying the trout. That large dorsal fin is marked with swirls and splashes of magenta and mauve. Her firm body is silver shot through with purples and lavender, studded with small flecks of black, shading from a smoky violet on the back through burnished silver to cream and gold on the belly. Colours which fade on death, which is reason alone to let such beauty slip back into the stream. Her pointed snout and underslung mouth show she lives on the stream bed in the fastest of flows. She has a strange pear-shaped eye and there, in the crease of her chin, is gold, washed down from the Welsh hills, gathered as she hugs the streambed; only the angler knows this.

She holds for a moment, hovering over the net, nose into the stream, unaware she is free. A slight movement and she pushes forward, sliding back to the stream. For such a splendid fish she disappears into the streambed when viewed from above, notoriously difficult to spot, much harder than the trout.

It feels good to catch that first fish, with any fish, even more so with grayling when there is the expectation that more will follow. The cast is checked and straightened and sent out to search for another. The flies drop into the slacker water on the far side of the main current and the rod is held high to lift the line off the flow and give the flies chance to trail across the slower water. Then, as they enter the faster deeper current, the bow in the line straightens as another grayling takes hold. Once more he heads for the depths. The rod is arched, bending, pointing to his position, but soon that dogged resistance is overcome and he can be steered to the side where the net awaits him.

Slightly smaller than the first, but no less welcome. The March Hare was his undoing; he is slipped back, a little wiser. The flies are sent out again and the same line carefully fished through. Again the same cast to the same position: grayling being a shoal fish will usually gather in some numbers. A searching cast, this time back upstream to find any fish missed before, with no result.

Move on a little downstream, the water here is less broken and a few rises have been seen. With less flow the Option 2 is taken off and a Burford Red knotted on. Straight away there is a tug and then nothing. Another cast produces another tug. These fish are just tweaking the fly, at times breaking the surface with a rise as they attack the fly skimming through. It seems these fish are 'pinks', very small immature grayling of six inches or so that often gather at the tail of the pool. Another cast confirms this as a little fish is flipped to the surface as he holds the fly a fraction too long. It seems because of the lower water levels, the pool contains fewer fish than normal. Time to move on. The next run is just a short wade away. Downstream the river's flow crosses to the far bank to give a deep run against a rocky outcrop. Weed beds at the head of the run give way to a strong, deep stream that always looks as if it should produce fish.

The flies go out to be caught in the current and swing around to fish downstream. The Burford Red is clipped on the lapel patch and the Option 2 has replaced it in the faster water. Second cast the line tightens and the rod bends. The line zips through the water as the fish runs downstream. This is no grayling: these are the dashing runs of a trout. Soon he comes to the surface the Option 2 fixed in his upper jaw. Surely he took it for an olive nymph dislodged from the weed bed. The March Hare dangles in mid-air hanging from the tight cast. A nice fish at about twelve inches. He comes in, mouth open, to be grasped by the lower jaw and the little nymph slid out. He goes into the record book. A few more days and his closed-season begins.

Out go the flies seeking the shoal of grayling. There is no response until the flies reach the deeper water where the run funnels between the rock ledge and the bank. There, in the shade of alder and hazel, are a few dimpling rises. Whereas in the shallow water only pinks and parr awaited the angler, these rises promise grayling of greater size. The Burford Red regains its position as the point fly: it will fish well as the river slows. A longer cast lands the flies on the far side of the run. The line is mended to keep contact. A rise, a swirl as the flies started to work across the flow, and a fish is on. Side strain quickly brings him away from the shoal and he kicks and fights in the side current. A nice fish, similar in size to the first, he is hussled into the waiting net and the Burford Red unhitched from his jaw. He swims away strongly. Another cast to the same spot brings another grayling, it seems the shoal has been found. The next cast produces a fish too, as does the next, all the fish are of a similar size, ten to twelve inches.

By now the centre of the pool is being covered, there are fewer rises here and a couple of casts go out without result. Time to rethink; the Option 2 can go on the point and the Burford Red moves up to the dropper. The cast goes out; a little ring shows where the weighted nymph lands.

Cast across the flow, the flies work around without reply. Cast again, the line is watched awaiting the lift in the curve signalling interest. Cast once more, following the flies, working them carefully across the current with a gentle nodding of the rod tip. The river flows by and somewhere in the trees a wood pigeon softly coos. A tap, no more, just a rap on the line, a sign that something alive is down there.

For the wet-fly fisherman the tug is the drug: that electric connection with another living thing in another element. Full concentration now, the flies go out to cover the same spot. Tap, the rod lifts and he is on. This feels like a better fish he stays deep and the rod is angled over to draw him away from the shoal. It is surprising sometimes just how many grayling can be caught from a shoal before they stop taking. Today the water is low and clear, the shoals less due to goosanders and cormorants, perhaps the day will return when twenty fish could be caught from a shoal, one day. Now the bent rod, tight line and sound of the reel as he twists and turns and takes line is enough. He is tiring now and the rod draws him, still struggling, into the side current where the net awaits. The Option 2 was only just clicked into his upper lip and falls out at the touch. He is a male, angry he squirms and furls his dorsal fin over his back, around fourteen inches, the biggest so far. The net sunk he swims away with a thrash of his tail and a spray of water. Straighten the line and check the tackle, wind knots and minor tangles are not immediately obvious, they go unnoticed until it is too late.

There is a smell, a smell of grayling. It gets on the hands of anglers lucky enough to handle them. Faint but distinctive it has led to them being given the Latin name of *Thymallus thymallus* although the smell is more metallic than herbal.

The flies go back out to seek another fish. The flow is less now towards the tail of the pool. There is a dark shelf of rock just showing. The line stops, no strike, no tug, simply stopped as if caught in weed, but there is no weed. A lift luckily hooks the grayling before he lets go. This time the fish is smaller, hooked on the Burford Red he is brought to the surface and quickly unhooked with an estimated ten inches recorded in the note book. Three further casts produce a pink and an end is called to further fishing as the shallow tail of the pool is reached.

There is another pool in this chain which holds fish and promises a few more to add to the tally. It is necessary to wade back up the run to get out of the river at the small gravel beach. Now turned and facing back upstream the going is more difficult, take small steps, it is easy to stumble. There are still a couple of fish rising. Two mallard fly in low and seeing their water occupied, fly away complaining. A grayling rises again in the main flow. Can the true angler resist a rising fish? In less than a minute the two wet flies are taken off and a Little Hereford knotted on to the tippet. The advantage of a nylon leader and floating line is the ability to switch quickly to a floating fly. The rise when it comes is slightly to the far side of the main flow. The first cast lands short and is quickly dragged away by the stream. Wade closer, the little size sixteen dun is flicked out again, a rise, and he's on. Another grayling comes tumbling back down the stream where he shows his annoyance at being fooled by splashing in the side stream. The line is held and, with rod tucked under arm, he is quickly unhooked in the water. A kingfisher darts up the river and perches on a branch on the far bank. In the shade he almost disappears, iridescent blue becomes grey in the shadows. He is halcyon, brought to life by the light of the sun.

The next pool is formed by the river flowing around large slabs of rock that jut out into the stream. Today with low water they are dry and, on the water-worn rock smoothed by years of floods, are holes, pock marks in the old sandstone, caused by 'turnstones', hard pebbles that settle into dips in the rock. Rattling and wobbling when the waters flow over, wearing their way deeper into the solid rock, until there remains a circular crater with a pebble at the bottom.

Now is the time to take a break. Sit the small wicker creel on the slabs and lay the rod down with fly hooked into the keeper ring. A steel flask holds hot sweet coffee. A drink, a chocolate bar and a few minutes to watch the river flow by. Far down the run, where the river slows and deepens, chub cruise and a few languid rises mark their presence. Water from waders trickles down the dry rock.

There are no rises, but on the bank a grey wagtail works his way along the water's edge, bobbing like a clockwork toy. Swap back to the wet-fly, the hackled spider patterns should work in the light flow. Snipe and Purple is a personal favourite, Partridge and Orange or a Silver March Brown work well too. A simpler version of the Silver March Brown, and easier to dress, is a Silver March Hare. It is simply a March Brown with a darker game bird hackle, grouse, woodcock or similar, and silver body. Grayling probably take these silver bodied flies for fry, the 'lady of the stream' will take small fish and can be caught on spinners. On the continent spinning is a recognised way of catching them, the tackle manufacturers

ABU produced small spinners and feathered lures recommended for grayling.

On the Teme the Red Tag is the fly everyone has heard of; first known as the Worcestershire Gem, however there are many other excellent local patterns. Personal preference counts for a lot. Anglers have favourite flies that get used frequently and in turn catch most fish.

The coffee is drained and the chocolate bar wrapper stowed in the creel. A cast of wet flies, lightly hackled 'spiders' is made up. A Snipe and Purple is tied on the dropper, just a wisp of a feather and a spot of colour but often a deadly grayling fly. On the point goes the Burford Red, a personal favourite. These lighter flies cast easily across the flow to cover the dimpling rises.

The flies go out; a short cast to cover the head of the run and the nearside bank. They provoke a rise mid-stream, just a rise, no fish. Try again. Follow the same line and let the flies linger slightly as they pass, bang, he's on. The rod kicks and becomes alive in the hand, steer him away from the flow, for a moment he holds himself against the strain of the line, the rod bent in a glorious curve, then with a dive he scythes across the stream to fight deep in the side current. A valiant fight, but he must yield to the rod's pressure as he twists and spins, and is gone. Just a slack line trails in the current. Strip it in, two tiny wakes in the water show the flies are still there. A check shows all is in order with the tackle. He simply slipped the hook. A pity, he felt like a good one too. It is disappointing, but in another minute he would have been unhooked and released anyway. It still hurts to lose a fish.

Grayling continue to rise in the run. Cast again, the flies settle and as the line is mended to keep contact, a fish rises and tweaks the line, he is on, the rod bends and then he's gone. Another chance is lost.

Again the flies go out. The arm has found its rhythm; the line lays on the water in a graceful curve. The rod tip tracks the course of the flies, the line hanging in a bow to the water. Tap, the line jerks and the rod is lifted into a fish. The rod again bends to the strain of the fish, he is downstream and backing away, kicking, and gone, (followed by a silent oath). Looking at the line dangling loosely in the stream it is easy to think that golf might be an easier option. Such foolishness lasts but seconds. In angling we are reminded that however smart and skilled we think we are, chance and nature always have the last word.

Once more check the tackle, all is in order, hooks sharp and straight. No sense in blaming the barbless hooks: such losses happen with barbed hooks too. Concentration is on the line as the flies work their way around. It takes half a dozen casts before the line stops mid-stream. The rod tip goes up and a grayling is hooked. A slightly smaller fish, he is quickly brought to the side and the little Snipe and Purple slipped from his lip.

A larger fish would add to the day. They are scarce, but no doubt a few exist down in the deepest runs and pools.

The flow quickens around the point of the rocks and in the deep channel the grayling lie close. Across the stream a fish rises, the grey wagtail flicks his tail and scampers across the rocks. The size sixteen Option 2 may work here, the extra weight should send it deeper and a gentle cast, slightly upstream, gives it time to drop through the water.

The rod held high guides the line around the rock, taking the pull of the current off the line so the tandem tungsten beads of the Option 2 take the flies to where the monsters may lie. Then, as the line is carried down the stream, a little line is let out to allow the flies to fish round. The cattle in the field opposite stop to watch, then deciding little of interest is happening, walk on.

The flies are retrieved and pitched again, slightly upstream. The rod tip follows their progress. There is a tap, a knock on the rod tip and the bow in the line straightens, a fish is on. Somewhere deep down a grayling is struggling, it feels a good fish. The rod takes on a healthy curve; the line quivers as it cuts through the current. He backs off downstream and for a moment line has to be given as the fish uses the heavy flow to put strain on the tackle. The soft check of the little Hardy Lightweight purrs, the music of the reel tells that a larger fish has been found. A finger on the spool acts as a brake to stop him taking too much line. Standing on the rocks it is impossible to get below him, it is unsettling having the grayling backing downstream twisting and spinning, straining hard against the line, at any time the hook hold might give and leave the angler holding nothing but his tongue and a slack line. This time all holds, the soft tip of the rod absorbs the shock and the fish tires enough to be steered out of the main stream. The line slants into the eddy where crab apples bob around in the flow. Down deep there is a silver gleam as the grayling turns. The rod maintains the pressure and a little more line can be wound back on the reel. Now he is under control. The net is readied, it is good to get him in once beaten. He dives trying to get back down to safety, instead he is turned and keeping pressure on brings him to the surface where, before he can dive again, the net is lifted around him.

A nice fish, male, the Option 2 is securely hooked in his rubbery lower lip. Freed, he lies in the net in the shallows, if picked up he would kick and squirm, it is better to let him catch his breath in the net. The balance shows his weight – after deducting for the net – at one pound and six ounces, a fine fish. A camera sits in the wader pocket, a photograph would be good. The rod is laid down, reel just over the net where the mesh is pulled back to reveal the fish. For a moment he lies flat. On a whim a couple of crab apples are scooped up and dropped next to him, and the picture taken. Squatting down on the rocks, holding the now empty net, the river reflects the blue sky and the dark trees, the wagtail is still hunting along the far bank and a fish rises. The flies are checked and another cast drops them into the stream, let's see if the trick can be repeated. A couple of casts produce nothing and with a few more fish dimpling the surface the mood changes from trying for a large fish deep down, to simply catching a few more fish.

To an angler there is no better feeling than that first contact with a fish, any fish. Whether he is a float fisherman, using a ledger, a spinner, or a fly, it is the moment he hooks the fish that is magic.

To work down the run it is necessary to get down from the rock slabs. Upstream, five feet of water awaits anyone who takes a step too far, while downstream, if careful, it is possible to find a way onto a shelf knee deep. Wading down alongside the run means casting is hampered by trees close behind, a roll cast, a Spey cast is useful here to send the flies across the stream. Wading and being closer to the water's surface brings into view details not seen before. Small light-coloured duns, pale-wateries or spur-wings, caught in the surface film, slip by.

The grayling rise close-by now and another grayling takes a size sixteen Snipe and Purple as it flickers across the flow. He dives and struggles under the rod tip, flashes of silver in the green depths, before he can be netted and released.

A few fish still rise across the stream ignoring the wet-fly even when it is fished with slack line to float down amongst them. Reach for the fly box; a tiny Gold-Ribbed Hare's Ear might work in this situation. It is nothing more than a pinch of fur ribbed with fine gold wire but it works like magic with grayling, and trout too. A look in the box shows a couple of Gold-Ribbed Hare's Ears, both matted and worn. It is the end of the year and the most useful flies are in short supply. Luckily a batch of Little Herefords have been dressed in anticipation of the grayling season and they sit in a neat rank ready to be dispatched. They will perch on the surface mimicking the high floating duns.

A size sixteen Little Hereford is tied on. It is an awkward cast across the flow, luckily the range is short. The fly drops on the stream and floats down, a little tuft of feather on the water. A second cast drops the fly amid the rises, across current it begins to drag but a fish is on, the fly taken as it landed. The line zips off the surface as contact is made, loose line is stripped in and the rod takes on a curve that shows a good fish is hooked, the rod bent full curve, angled over to the side, straining against the fish fighting in the stream, he kicks and rolls, each action pulling the rod around, the line stretching into the deep, the insistent pull of the rod takes its toll and the grayling comes tumbling out of the main flow into the side stream, without the strength of the flow he is quickly under control, held by the rod. Time to get him into the net. Shorten the line and get his head up. He comes in and the net raised. He fought well. In the net he doesn't look so large. The balance shows him to be two ounces short of a pound. The net is lowered and he glides over the rim and back to the stream.

There are still a couple of fish rising so let's see if we can repeat the trick. The casting is tight and the fly, instead of covering the grayling, seeks sanctuary in a hazel branch. The day is going on, the casting arm is tired, mistakes are beginning to creep in, twigs are removed to free the line. Try again. This time the fly lands in the flow and is whisked away. A little more line and at last the fly alights in the target area with a little slack line. The tuft of cul-de-canard stands out, a dot on the water. Fish rise nearby but it takes two more casts before another grayling comes to the fly. The rod goes up and he is hooked. A smaller fish this, he is bundled across the mainstream before he has chance to struggle then, head up, brought to hand. Hooked lightly in the upper jaw, the barbless hook can be removed without lifting him from the water. The sun is low in the western sky: the warmth is going out of the day. With the day much cooler, and the sun off the water, it is reluctantly time to finish. Wade back to the slabs, sit awhile and have a last cup of coffee.

Across the fields another fisherman is heading home to the heronry at Berrington Hall. It has been a good day. Looking in the notebook the tally shows sixteen grayling up to one pound six ounces

By Onny, Teme and Clun

and a bonus trout. Numbers don't equal happiness, but there is a satisfaction in looking back on a good 'bag'.

WINTER

One word on fishing in winter. Don't.

To everything there is a season and winter is the season for fly dressing and books.

The Teme regularly floods towards the tail end of the year and the grayling fisher is often frustrated that he cannot fish much beyond November. The river rises with the late autumnal rains and runs high if not flooded through until spring.

No doubt someone has had a wonderful day on the Teme when the weather was so bad Captain Oates would have stayed inside, but not that I've heard of.

Angling, and especially fly-fishing, is a gentle art. It is enjoyable to cast a line in the warmer months of the year when conditions are comfortable. It should never be a test of endurance. There comes a time when even the most enthusiastic angler must admit that the best is over, or the river will call time by coming down in a red flood. Then it is time to rule a line in the diary and count up your blessings.

On the river the fish are still there, even in the worst floods they are tucked tight into the banks. For the angler it is the tail-end of the year but, for the trout gathering on the gravels, it is a new beginning and new life is hidden under the pebbles awaiting the warmth of spring.

The angler in winter, apart from the occasional walk to stretch his legs or a little log cutting, will find the months of December, January and February are much better spent by the fireside in the construction of flies or repair of tackle, or reading a good book.

For some winter can be a disheartening time; it may help to jot down things to enjoy in the wintertime. Suggestions could include, toasted teacakes, hot mugs of coffee after a brisk walk, or a personal favourite, log fires. Wood smoke was described by John Betjeman as the 'Scented luxury of life', anyone fortunate enough to be looking to buy a property in the Teme valley should stipulate, along with the number of bedrooms, the warmth of a log fire, for a house is less without it.

CLOSED-SEASON

The closed-season is for most anglers a period to spend time in the bosom of their family, without the nagging call of the river. The odd jobs that were put off when the trout were rising, those outstanding tasks can now be completed.

They may not always be the ones that the lady of the house was expecting. Those shelves may have to wait a little longer as March Browns are in short supply in the fly box, and fixing that sticking drawer be postponed as that squirrel pelt a fellow angler donated simply must be tried in an emerger pattern.

No matter what, the angler will be 'at home'. For that his family should be grateful. The lady of the house complained bitterly that, on every balmy summer's eve, her man was absent and for long periods when the mayfly hatched he was but a myth, both at the office and the home. Now she has him in residence full time. Children may tug nervously at mummy's apron and whisper 'Who is that funny man?' But he will be at hand to tuck them in at night with a bedtime story, and soon they will become familiar with the exploits of Mr Crabtree and Peter.

Homework too will come readily to the once missing father, physics explained in terms of test curves and breaking strains; biology clarified with a brief talk on entomology, with particular emphasis on the merits of the lesser olives over the mayfly. While history is enlivened by reopening the 1938 debates between the supporters of Halford and Skues on the ethics of nymph fishing on chalkstreams.

The angler can settle back into the marital home in a state of bliss, assured that the dining room table will be cleared of rods by March, or April at the latest. The fly lines, wound around the dining room chairs, and the drying rows of bright floats looking so gay in their fresh coats of paint, can then come down to be neatly stored away in the tackle box which sits handily in the corner of the living room. The lady of the house may now be so impressed with his attendance that she may wish to reward him with the promise of a day's fishing as the new season approaches. She may ask 'Just when does the season start?'

One blessing of the closed-season is the anticipation of the opening day. The first day of the season is awaited with the same eagerness as Christmas by a nine-year-old. Days are counted off as tackle is prepared and plans made. When the day arrives there is hope as the angler sets out and should he return with no great prize to record, then there is no cause for concern, for isn't the whole season stretching out ahead?

Each time our hope is renewed and when that glorious day dawns and we head down to the waterside, given an extra sparkle by the closed-season, it is to meet an old friend as familiar as a well-worn pair of brogues. No golfer will experience such joy.

Yet the new season is not really new. It is a renewal of our relationship with the river. An annual refreshing of our union when, for every new thing we try out, there are many well-loved and well-learnt ways to which we return. Layers laid upon layers to give greater depth to our angling.

Remember, to season is to add spice and the seasoned angler has knowledge and experience. Seasoning our angling year brings out its true flavour.

To persist without pause risks the mindless repetition of mechanical actions. Part of the romance of angling is the anticipation that makes the arrival of the new season all the more enjoyable. Our appetite would become jaded if there were a constant availability of angling days.

There are changes of course, what we want from angling changes over the seasons. The river changes year by year. The changes are subtle and year by year like old friends we settle together in our intimate relationship. Without a closed-season these vicissitudes could be lost in a continuous blur. The closed-season highlights the slight changes and gives the angler a chance to stand back and assess what he does.

The border angler may be familiar with the Welsh word, Hiraeth, meaning a deep longing for, especially for home. There is no equivalent in the English language, but the angler in the closed-season will know it.

Closed season

Although the open season for grayling is longer than that for trout, on the Teme November floods often limit any advantage the bait fisherman might expect. It is a rare day when the angler can expect sport in winter. With the trout season off to an early start in spring, the opportunity to fish for either is fairly equal.

However, no season need be barren of pleasure. What then to do when kept away from the waterside? The obvious thing is to read. Books are fireside fishing, a winter sport that has much to recommend it. It is perhaps because of the long closed-season that the angler has the greatest library of any pastime. It enriches our sport and encourages the angler to think a little more deeply into what he does.

Consider a shelf full of books on angling, what hours of work have gone into those, what stories, what days by what rivers. If all that knowledge could be absorbed by the angler what fish he would catch; maybe.

With fly-dressing and tackle repair in the winter months, there is probably not a time when the angler cannot be immersed in angling. Like a glass of port after a fine meal, autumn is the time to savour the season past. In winter he may, in his mind's eye, fish again those sparkling streams of happy memory. To avoid over fishing a closed-season he, like Sir Edward Grey, may restrict his imaginary angling until the New Year has passed. Of more practical and pragmatic concern is the state of tackle after a season's work. Wet autumn banks have left rods and reels muddy, nets damp and with an unwelcome odour not appreciated by the lady of the house. One of the drawbacks of modern tackle is that it needs little maintenance, but there is still work that can be done. The angler with cane rods has the opportunity to varnish or even rewhip rods over the winter months. It is likely he may have discovered an old rod in a second-hand shop, then real work can commence. Success in angling often relies on the accumulation of many small factors; losses are often the result of one. Now is the time to check and recheck all is in order.

So the angler may varnish rods. He also oils his reels, checks and replaces lines, even repaints floats in bright and jolly colours and imagines them

Closed season

disappearing from sight on some bright and sunny day. The trout fisher has his flies, but the all-round angler dreams on dark evenings of the red-tipped quill bobbing and gliding away by the lily pads, or the orange topped cork waltzing and curtsying carried down some deep swift run. The fly-fisher regards his ranks of flies as an army set to meet the current and lure the fighting trout to the surface. Both look upon these tools of their sport with pleasure, (it is their disappearance that will give the greater pleasure).

Maybe the fly-fisher has the better deal, as there are only so many floats that you may make excuse for, whereas the fly-fisher dresses his flies by the dozen and with good reason. One fly is for the far bank alders, one is to be snapped off on the fence behind, one dropped in the grass never to be found, the list goes on. True, he turns out the flies successful last year, although there are always those patterns recommended by friends, and books. He may have managed without an emerger pattern for a blue-winged olive hatch but, having read this month's edition of 'Hook 'em' magazine, he wonders at the fool he has been for not thinking of it before and immediately ties up a dozen of the latest 'deadly fish taker'. There it sits on the table, perched on the polished surface on tail and hackle tips, irresistible. A fly that will succeed in any situation. He cannot wait to tie it on. The very table top rocks as the trout's nose breaks through to take it off the surface.

ON RODS

Here are some thoughts and ideas on suitable fly rods for those coming to fish the rivers and streams of the Teme valley. The experienced angler, with a selection of rods for his home waters, will know the importance of having tackle suitable for each. The still-water angler and those fishing differing rivers will want to know how suitable their rods may be if transferred to the border streams. The novice, who by lucky chance may find these streams his local waters, may need guidance on choice of rod.

Tackle advertisements tempt novices to buy success. They promise the latest rod will improve your performance, when truly that will only come with practice, at no cost but time. It is inviting to believe that better tackle brings instant rewards, but, alas, it rarely does. To begin with, use sound basic tackle and make use of any spare cash to access better waters on which to practice.

Our border streams and rivers are not at the forefront of tackle manufacturers minds and many of their products are aimed at still-waters or wide, open chalk-streams. Fortunately, in amongst the dozens of models of rods offered for sale, there are some ideally suited to these small streams.

We are fortunate to be living in a 'Golden Age' when it comes to fishing tackle. Technical advances in materials and manufacturing, along with mass production and competition, are producing rods of superb quality and specification at very low price. Any of the 'bargain' rods sold by the main manufacturers will give the angler many years of useful service. Marketing strategy means that tackle manufacturers sell their 'entry level' rods at prices little above cost, in an effort to encourage anglers to continue buying higher priced models.

As the angling opportunities in the area are so diverse, from the wide gravel runs of the main river to the jungle like conditions of the smaller streams, a selection of rods is the ideal. Therefore it makes sense to choose the discount or bargain rod, and avoid the temptation of anything of a higher grade in order to afford an additional rod of different length later on. Several rods of say seven, eight and nine feet will be much more useful than just one more expensive. So, given that a decent rod may be obtained cheaply, the main consideration is length.

Length

The varying conditions and various rivers ideally require different lengths of rod. Various telescopic rods and rods that make up into combinations of lengths and actions have been made, none were popular and for good reason. The angler, having saved money with an inexpensive rod, will find a second or third rod of differing length will be a good use for his savings.

For a good general rod, a length of eight feet will do nicely. It will enable the angler to fish the main river and streams, wet or dry fly in all styles and methods. While it may not be ideal for the more specialist techniques, it will do. Eight feet is the starter for the novice and will allow him to fish happily on most of the waters.

The next rod in the armoury depends on the waters being most regularly fished. Let us suppose the angler wants to fish the Rivers Arrow, Clun,

Corve or Ledwyche in some of their overgrown sections. While he will manage with his eight-foot rod on many sections, there will be some where it will be frustrating to try to cast between overgrown banks and overhanging trees. Then a short rod of seven feet would be better. Avoid going too short, a six-foot rod may look and feel nice but control over the line when casting, lifting the line and striking is very limited.

For the main river a nine-foot rod is a nice choice. A lot of trout and grayling fishing on the Teme takes place on the faster waters, the shallows or fords. Here a longer rod is no problem and will give better line control, better control over the fly. For the novice it should be said that the use of a longer rod is not to handle bigger fish or cast further, it is simply to control the line and fly more easily. Line control is especially important when wet-fly fishing or fishing with bugs or nymphs. Specialist rods for this style of fishing can be ten or eleven feet, you may consider that later; for a start, a nine-foot rod is sufficient.

A final note on rod length is the need for a shorter rod as the season progresses. Even when

On Rods

fishing the same sections of river, you may find a shorter rod is needed in the summer months. The reason is quite simple. In the early spring you will be fishing from almost bare banks, vegetation will be minimal. However a seven foot rod might be your choice in summer to fit between nettle beds and overhanging branches. In March and April, an eight-foot rod will give better control over deep nymphs and wet flies on the more open banks of springtime. It is useful to make note of the best length of rod for the stretches fished. A short rod may hinder casting and hamper line control, but too long a rod can drive you to madness. There are few things more frustrating than finding a good rise on a stream not fished for a time, only to realise the eight-foot rod you've bought continually catches up in the summer vegetation and the seven foot is what is needed. There speaks experience.

Line-weight

Now line-weight. Each rod will be rated for a weight of line. The typical eight-foot rod, taken as the starting point, may be rated 8ft-4 weight (or 4#), this simply means that the rods action is suited to a four-weight line. Trout fly lines come in sizes one to ten, with the most usable sizes three to six weight. You need a line to match the rod (see section on lines). The four-weight line, with rod to match, is a good start on most rivers and small streams. Some rods are rated with two line numbers thus 4/5#. This is the range that we are looking at, 3/4 # would also be suitable. You may read that a rod used only for short casts needs to have a line one size heavier to compensate for the short line, this may work but I suggest the novice sticks with the suggested line-weight for the rod and fine tunes the detail later. Rods casting a six weight line or above are really too powerful. Novices should be wary of advice that it will cast further or easier, long casts are seldom needed, lightness and precision are. Still-water anglers may utilise a nine-foot six weight rod on the river until they find something more suitable and even a ten or eleven foot, light line rod may be useful for wet-fly or nymph fishing. Generally, the chalk-stream rod may be too long to tackle the small streams, although fine on the main river.

Action

The other side of rod performance is 'action'. While a rod may be lightweight and work well with a fairly light line of three or four weight, it may have its 'flex' or action in the top quarter of the rod. Such an action, known as a 'fast' action helps create high line speeds, and possibly, accurate casts. This is the action needed for casting into the wind, especially when trying to gain extra distance on large still-waters. Opinions vary, and personal preference comes into play, but generally, for the novice and those new to fishing the border streams, a fast action is not needed. The windswept bank of the reservoir may require a line to be punched out, small streams do not. Gentle presentation is far more valuable than power. It is not a thing to fret over, but do not especially seek out a fast action rod. The alternative 'through action' or 'full flex', where the rod bends throughout its length, is ideal for the smaller rivers and streams of the area. Apart from a gentle presentation, the through action will let you roll, flick, switch, sweep and swing your line in all the odd casts that overgrown waters demand. A through action is far more forgiving when the timing of the cast is less than perfect, and there will be many times on an overgrown stream when your timing is hampered. A through or easy action, even if a little 'soft', is ideal for the small streams and small trout of the Teme valley.

Materials

Most rods sold now are made from carbon fibre. The novice need look no further. Carbon fibre rods are inexpensive, light, and robust. Carbon fibre, also known as graphite, rods are the most common for very good reasons and they are perfectly acceptable and adequate tools for the job.

However, the angler will know angling is not about the merely functional, there is an element of art. While the novice should start with the basic outfit, and he will find test enough in our streams, there will come a time when he considers split-cane. Some fish with cane rods because it amuses them. Simple sensible considerations are not all, while the head may choose the practical, the heart may lead you to a rod you consider a thing of beauty. The angler will want to be pleased with what he has. A rod is far more than simply a tool for doing a job. Rather like a magician's wand or a conductor's baton, a rod will conjure up great things. A rod made from a natural material not only looks lovely, but also feels good in the hand. As you may hold your rod for longer than your wife, a similar careful choice should be made.

Split-cane makes a lovely rod and does have some advantages on a small stream. As a material, cane is less stiff, size for size, than carbon fibre. Carbon fibre rods can be made much thinner, and lighter, than a cane rod and still have the same stiff springy action needed to cast a fly. Although the same volume of carbon fibre is nearly three times as heavy as cane, because much less material (volume) is needed, carbon fibre rods are much lighter. This benefit of a lighter rod is particularly noticeable on lakes and reservoirs where longer rods are used and a stiff, powerful rod produces long casts, often against the wind. The advantages of carbon fibre rods are compounded for these situations, and, as the majority of rods were produced for still-waters, they are commonplace.

With small streams the advantages of carbon fibre are less clear. Small stream rods are shorter so the weight difference is small. They cast lighter lines shorter distances, so less material is used to give them the action needed, weight difference becomes marginal. Whereas a nine- or ten-foot cane rod used for continuous still-water casting may be impractical, a small stream seven- or eight-foot split-cane rod is a joy.

Weight is not always obvious. A well-balanced rod feels light in the hand. Even a light-weight rod, if unbalanced in the hand, will feel heavy and tire the user.

The softer, less stiff, nature of cane can work to advantage on smaller waters. If an angler in his local tackle shop picks up a carbon fibre rod and waggles it in the air, as some do, he finds little happens. The rod hardly flexes without a length, and weight, of line out through the rings. If his local tackle shop sold cane rods, he would find the same length of rod would flex and bend as he waved it. The reason is twofold, cane is naturally more flexible and supple, thus the extra material needed to stiffen it makes it heavier; this inbuilt weight causes the cane rod to flex with no line attached. The rod feels as if there is a line on it already. The advantage for some small stream fishing is that the rod will flex and throw a line with very little line beyond the rod tip. This ability to work with very little line extended is an asset when using cane rods in tight corners.

The slower, softer nature of the cane rod is ideal for the small stream. The combination of odd casts which send the fly under bushes, through gaps and around corners, calls for a forgiving easy action. With practice, you will be able to lay the lines up a tunnel of bushes that looks impossibly narrow, using the rod to stroke out a cast like an artist using a brush.

Of course, there is a downside to obtaining a split-cane rod. New split-cane rods are individually handcrafted and very expensive. Prices for new rods can be ten or twenty times the cost of an economy carbon fibre rod. Some split-cane is available as blanks or kits to be made up, although not cheap and requiring some skill, it is an alternative. A better alternative for those with limited budgets is to buy second-hand.

For the novice there may be some confusion over the terms cane, split-cane and built cane. Cane is a name for the hollow stem of tall reeds and grasses. Bamboo is the type of cane used for fishing rods. Some longer bait rods use whole cane in the bottom joints where less flexibility is required. Most fly rods are of split-cane. Technically, large whole canes are split to provide strips which are glued together to give the hexagonal shape characteristic of cane rods. A cheaper or quicker alternative is to cut or saw the strips instead of splitting them, the result (built-cane) being considered by some to be inferior. It is difficult to tell, some cheap continental or Asian made rods are out there, but try it out and if it is the right length, action and price, the choice is yours.

There are other materials of course. Glass fibre was popular in the nineteen sixties and seventies. A good glass fibre rod is fine, heavier than carbon fibre length for length, and perhaps not as good looking as cane. Again novices will find little advantage, but the experienced angler may want to try it out.

On Rods

Older and rarer is greenheart, a solid wood from British Guyana, South America. It was used for rods back in Victorian times and out-dated by mid-twentieth century. Even heavier than cane length for length, only short rods are practical. It looks like a varnished mahogany rod and is quite brittle especially when old; not for everyday use. Only for anglers with a taste for the esoteric; I have one.

Details

The number of sections that the rod can be broken down into is normally not important. The more joints, the greater potential for wear and damage, but these problems are rare on carbon fibre rods. More joints can add weight and introduce flat spots in the curve, again negligible in carbon fibre rods. On the positive side, the more joints the shorter the sections, making it handy to drop into the back seat of the car. Personal preference and availability will guide the angler, the choice will make little difference to suitability to fishing border streams.

A keeper ring, the small ring or loop just above the handle, is useful on all rods and almost essential on fly rods. Attaching the hook to the bottom ring is inconvenient and may damage the ring or its lining. If your rod doesn't have a keeper ring, a perfectly good one may be made from a paperclip and whipped on.

When transporting rods some sort of protection is needed. Modern rods sometimes come in tubes. An alternative is to use black plastic rainwater downpipes from a D.I.Y store or fishing tackle shops. A rod bag is still needed to stop scratches.

If you fish after work you may need to use a carbon fibre rod, a cane rod will suffer waiting in the heat of the car. Another way a cane rod will suffer is if the angler tugs the line using the rod when the fly snags; always release pressure and untangle or pull by hand. Carbon fibre is tough, but cane will fracture or be damaged.

Finally, remember the old saying that fools lay their rods on the ground, for greater fools to tread on them.

ON REELS

When choosing a fly reel for the small streams and rivers of the Welsh Marches, a novice will perhaps ask. 'Can I use the one I already have?' Probably yes. A good general-purpose reel is fine on small streams.

If for some reason a new reel is needed, the choice of an ideal reel would be something a little over three inches in diameter, and lightweight. There are some very small, light reels sometimes advertised as small stream or brook reels for light lines. They look wonderful, like little jewels, but a problem is winding in line on these mini reels takes time. After a strike recovering loose line may take too much time, and any slack might lose you the fish.

Very small reels also confine the line in tight coils so the line tends to come off the reel in a long spiral which hampers casting.

To increase the spool diameter on any reel, even when empty, backing is used. Experts may say that the backing is to allow you to keep contact with your fish as it races off with all your fly line and keeps going. What they have in mind are the Bonefish off the Florida Keys; a fish that takes all the fly line and runs into the backing on a small stream will end up in the field opposite.

For many years I fished with baler twine as backing to bring up the diameter of my reel. I only changed it because I got fed up with the bright orange colour.

The reel is always recommended to 'balance' the rod. For a lightweight carbon fibre rod a lightweight reel is the ideal. It will reduce fatigue, not just because it is lighter to hold, but it also has less momentum to stop and change direction as it swings through the casting stroke. Older cane rods typically had older heavier reels and this helps to balance the outfit. The heavier rod in front and the heavier reel behind the hand, means the balance point is now nearer to your grip. A lightweight reel can make a cane rod feel front heavy. Don't neglect older serviceable reels, especially with cane rods.

Reels are often advertised with sophisticated drags or braking systems. You may need disc brakes to slow your Ferrari, but a twelve inch brown trout rarely reaches such speeds. An exposed rim is handy, just to put your finger against, maybe, but complex drags and brakes are not really needed.

Which brings us to checks, all reels have some sort of check, it is there to stop the reel overrunning. Probably the simplest and commonest check is a ratchet type. The fly-fishing reel is the only item of tackle which makes a noise. At the waterside the only noise you want to hear is a tinkling stream, birdsong, and perhaps the soft purr of a well-oiled reel, a precision piece of equipment, as you pull line off before that carefully judged cast to a rising trout. Think of the honeyed tones of Joanna Lumley whispering in your ear, that sort of thing. What you do not need is a raucous clatter that sounds more like a marble in a baked bean can. No doubt tackle collectors can identify various Hardy reels just by the sound they make. I have a little Hardy Lightweight that purrs. So always check the check, some otherwise nice reels sound awful. So if you have a reel that sounds more Motorhead than Mozart, what can you do? Most spring check reels have a pawl (clicker) that comes out easily and, by gently filing the sharp point off, you can quieten the sound. I wouldn't do it with a priceless Hardy, but it makes a cheap reel sound much better. An alternative with an expensive reel is to get a five-millimetre-thick hard plastic sheet and cut out a replacement pawl. It works if you lose the pawl too.

Anglers now are in the lucky position of having a good choice of cheap but well-made reels. It does not have to cost a lot to have a nice reel. Check second hand reels, there are some good reels to be had for just a few pounds. Keep it simple, listen to it, and if you are happy with it, use it.

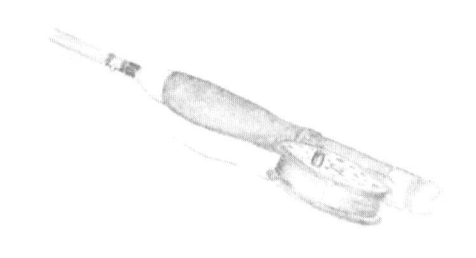

ON LINES, LEADERS, AND TIPPETS

Lines

A fly line is an expensive item that has to be bought new and may cost the equivalent of a cheap rod. Here are a few suggestions on lines particularly applicable to border streams.

The line weight will need to match your rod. A second-hand split-cane rod may have no recommendation marked on it. Try borrowing a reel and line and testing it. Four or Five weight is a typical starting point. Cane rods are quite forgiving and accommodate a wide range of line weights.

First choice is, a floating or sinking line? A floating line can deal with every normal eventuality on border rivers and streams. Whereas sinking lines are suited to larger deeper waters, so floating it is.

Second choice is, double taper or weight forward line? Weight forward lines were developed to assist casting distances on still-waters due to the reduced friction of the thinner running line. On small rivers and streams this is rarely an advantage and it has many disadvantages. A weight forward line is harder to roll cast, harder to mend line with, harder to make delicate presentations, and costs twice as much (as double taper lines can be reversed). All these are important and disadvantages outweigh any advantage they may have. Some anglers prefer weight forward lines, it is their choice at the end of the day.

A note here, if any novice thinks that roll casts are beyond him, a few seasons on small streams, where he will use every type of cast, some with names, some without and some with names not to be repeated here, will teach him. They will become second nature, he will learn by practice and necessity to hold line back, shoot it in low, held high, tucks, drops, and switches, a double taper line will cope with them all.

Third choice is colour of the fly line. Most fly lines are a bright colour. The reason given for this is that it makes them easier to see. The person who has difficulty in seeing the end of a fly line is likely to be the still-water angler who is troubled with difficult light on the water and who needs to watch the end of his fly line for takes. This is of little consequence on a small stream where the tip of the flyline is only a few metres away. Most of the time the angler on border streams will be watching a dry fly, or a fly just under the surface, when a take can be seen. Even when the angler is fishing deep with a nymph, the leader is the indicator, if the angler waited until the fly line moved, they would miss most takes.

On a small stream the need is for stealth and concealment. Some argue that light lines are better because the fish see them against the light sky. If that were the case surely they would only see a silhouette, so colour wouldn't matter. As most of the streams fished are overhung or bordered by trees then the fly line, if seen at all, is seen against a dark background, so a dark line is less obvious. If you need to spot your fishing companion just watch out when he casts, that light coloured line can be seen a field away. These bright lines of fluorescent orange or acid green jar with the tranquil and subtle shades of the waterside. Most things that float down the river, twigs and debris are dark, so a dark fly line makes sense. Fly lines can be found in darker colours, straw, various greens, and even a dark olive. They may give an advantage of concealment.

Finally, always wipe or wash your fingers after using anti-midge cream, as some have ingredients that can harm fly-lines, plus you risk alerting the fish with a strange smell.

Leaders

The next link is the leader, the tapered section of monofilament that connects the fly line to the tippet.

Anglers sometimes use various thicknesses of nylon to tie a length of leader stepping down from thickest to thinnest. Braided monofilament leaders are also available; however, a simple shop bought tapered leader works fine. The taper is sometimes shown as steep taper or standard, either will do.

As to length, 9 feet is about standard. You may wish to go shorter for small overgrown streams, then 6 feet could be a minimum, or longer, for wide Teme fords or spooky trout on calm evenings, up to 12 feet if you can manage it. A rule of thumb measurement is to hold one end pinched between thumb and finger and stretch out your arm until at full span. Bring the leader to your nose, that is near enough a yard or a metre. Do it twice you have 6 feet (2 yards), a very short leader. Do it three times you have 9 feet (3 yards) an average leader, four times equals a long leader, simple.

Final breaking strain is usually in the range 3lb-5lb with the final reduction being provided by the tippet.

Once the leader and tippet are tied on you may find the thick nylon of the leader has set in coils like a giant spring. Holding the tippet, loop your line around a smooth fence post and stretch it straight, - that may also reveal a weak knot.

Material is usually nylon monofilament of some type, either completely clear or a pale green. An alternative monofilament exists in the form of Fluorocarbon. Fluorocarbon monofilaments have few advantages in our small streams. Fluorocarbons (or Fluro) sink more quickly than nylon. In practice this is hardly noticeable when using it for tippets in fine diameters. Thicker sections used for leaders sink more readily, so are a problem for dry fly fishing or where you may switch from one method to another. Fast sink rate is an advantage to the still-water fisher, but not on these streams. The other advantage put forward is that it is less visible under water, again an advantage to the still-water fisher rather than on the streams.

The main disadvantage is that the stuff never rots. Nylon will weaken and decay after a few years, fluorocarbon never does. No one knows how long it stays in the environment, possibly thousands of years, a frightening thought. Personally, I am more concerned for wildlife and the environment than the chance of an extra fish.

Tippets

The short section of level nylon line that joins the leader to the fly, was called the cast or the point, is now is usually called the tippet, available in different materials, the main ones being nylon of various forms and Fluorocarbon. Both will float if they are greasy and sink when they are dirty. Nylon left on the river bank kills wildlife and can remain dangerous for years before it decays. Fluorocarbon left on the river bank kills wildlife and no one is sure how long it will be before it decays, some estimates say thousands of years. Up to you.

Nylon works well as a tippet material, strong for its diameter and in various translucent colours. Knots between fluorocarbon and nylon are problematical, so be aware and use a tippet ring. When choosing tippet the practical considerations are thickness and strength, we want fine and strong.

Testing popular tippet materials, I found that generally the diameter or thickness as printed on the front of the spool was correct. The line diameter was tested using a digital Vernier dial gauge. However, there were vast discrepancies in the strength as tested. Using a spring balance and a fixed point, the line was strained until it broke. Loops were tied each end using a four-turn water knot; these never broke which gives confidence in the knot. The line broke each time mid-way. No doubt someone will tell me that the method wasn't scientific, but the plain nylon broke consistently near to the stated breaking strain, whereas some fluorocarbons broke at much less. Some very expensive fluorocarbon broke at half the stated breaking strain. Try it yourself.

You may use a good, cheap nylon: the stuff used for coarse fishing is fine. Tippet material just comes on better spools.

Three pound breaking strain would be a good start, granted the trout are not likely to exceed one pound, but they might. Importantly for border anglers, you will be forever snapping off flies in the bushes if you use light line. Three pound will give you a chance of retrieving the fly.

If in high summer you find that tiny flies don't fish well on regular line, scale down to two-pound breaking strain. Match the tippet to fly size. At mayfly time, or when using heavy nymphs, step up the strength, six pound breaking strain is not too much. Big flies turn over better with heavier nylon. Bushy or heavy flies can 'hinge' the nylon and weaken it at the hook eye.

The other frequent cause of weakness is a wind knot, a simple overhand knot commonly found when casting into the wind. Never fish with a wind knot in your leader. To show how it weakens the line, attempt breaking six pound breaking strain

On Lines, Leaders and Tippets

line with your hands, you won't. Now tie a simple overhand knot in it, and attempt it, easy.

Test your line from time to time, before a fish of a lifetime does.

ON KNOTS AND TANGLES

The dictionary defines a knot as 'a complication of threads formed by entangling', it sounds rather daunting, knots should not be. Perhaps 'to secure by fastening' makes better sense. To misquote Mark Twain, 'A knot is just a tangle with a college education'.

Every angler should be able to tie a few basic knots, practice until you can tie them consistently and confidently. End tackle at its simplest is a line and a hook, the hook being a fly if you wish. At all times the line must be in proportion to the hook, very fine line tied to a large hook may slip.

To tie the hook to the line a useful knot is the half-blood knot, quick and simple to tie, even quicker to undo, and rarely fails.

The knot is best shown in a drawing and there are plenty of illustrations to be found, but basically it consists of threading the line through the eye of the hook, twisting the short end back up the line four or five times and then poking the end through the loop made next to the eye.

On Knots and Tangles

Tied in this way it is possible to pinch with your finger nails the turns next to the eye and pull the knot apart, which is handy if you want to change flies frequently. It very rarely fails if tied and tightened properly. If you are after Teme barbel the tucked version, where the tail is tucked back in, might be better; that version doesn't pull apart. For very large Teme barbel you may also wish to test your knots and line with a spring balance.

If this knot only was used, it would be possible to fish quite effectively. The hook length, or tippet in fly-fisher's terms, could be tied to the hook with a half blood, and the other end tied to a little ring, called a tippet ring, leader ring, or rig ring depending on your fancy, they are all the same. With the leader tied to the ring, you are ready to go dry fly fishing, simply add a short length of line to the ring. Using the same knot, add droppers to the ring and you are rigged for wet-fly, a simple and strong set up. The rings, even the small ones, are much stronger than the line and they weigh next to nothing.

This basic set up works for bait fishing too. The hook length can be your favourite material and reduced breaking strain from the main line, simply to avoid leaving a long length of line in case of breakages. The bigger rings act as good stops for a running weight, or an attachment point for a paternoster or link weight. It is no problem for float fishing as the float rubbers will slip over it. Rings are useful to avoid tying fluorocarbon directly to nylon, which is unreliable.

The traditional way of joining two lengths of line is the blood knot, which is two half-blood knots back to back, but I suspect you were ahead of me there. It is a good knot, but really you need three hands and your teeth to tighten it properly. A simpler solution is to join two loops. Each line has a loop tied to the end, and the loop on the short length is threaded through the loop on the main line and the short line threaded through itself, then pulled tight. To tie the loops, double the line and then circle the doubled line around on itself, twist the looped end through itself four times, pull tight, you have a four-turn water knot. If you 'roll' the circled line forwards you can get small neat loops.

On Knots and Tangles

The only other knot that I have used is what I know as the Grinner knot, but is very similar to, and confused with, several other knots.

Knots seem to be difficult to define and often go by several names. Accidental knots have even more names, few of which can be repeated here.

For a Grinner, as I know it, thread line through the eye, pull a good length of line through and double it back on itself alongside the main line, and wind the free end back up around the doubled section four times before threading it through the loop of the doubled line, pull tight. The advantage of this knot is that the knot will tighten but using finger nails it is easy to slacken the noose that would hold the hook eye tight thus allowing the hook to hinge. This is considered an advantage by some experienced salmon fishermen who say the fly swims better in this loose hold, wet-fly fishers may agree. When I showed this to some other salmon fishers they said no, the fly should be tied on with a special knot that ensures the fly is always held in line and doesn't hinge. This probably says more about salmon fishermen than about knots.

An alternative to a knot is a splice. A knotless tapered leader can be attached to a fly-line by a glued splice.

Push a fine needle up the end of the fly-line as far as possible (about 1"/25mm). When it will go no further, bend the line to bring the needle point out through the side. Press the needle in to enlarge the hole. Remove the needle.

The last 1"/25mm or so of the fly-line should now be hollow with a sharp bend and hole where the point of the needle emerged. Thread your leader, thin end first, into the hole to emerge through the end of the fly-line. Pull it almost through.

Roughen the last 6"/150mm of the thick end of the leader with sandpaper or a file to provide a key (grip) for the glue. Then cover this section with a waterproof iso-cyanate (super) glue. Draw this last section into the fly-line. It should bond instantly. Test it. If it fails, snip off and try again.

Soak everything under water to set any remaining glue and trim off.

You now have a smooth join that will slide easily through the top ring. Useful when using short, small-stream rods and long leaders. While it doesn't come with a guarantee, I have used it for years without mishap.

Tangles

One definition of a tangle is, 'to twist together into a knotted mass', something with which anglers will be familiar. Anglers will also understand the term 'tangling with' and its meaning to 'come into conflict', both are things to be avoided. Those with a classical and philosophical leaning may consider tangles and wind-knots to be jokes sent by Aeolus[5] to test mortals.

Tangles beget tangles. When the fly is tugged by mischievous Puck, the imp who sits in alder trees and catches flies, stop. Examine your nylon. You will see that in less than a second it has been woven into the aforementioned knotted mass. How this happens, no one knows. At the first sign of a tangle, wind in and check. To ignore it and carry on casting will surely bring you 'into conflict'; tangles beget tangles.

---

[5] Greek god of wind.

Take a deep breath and go for your fid. Besides a good scrabble word, a fid is a knot picker. Any smooth, sharp pointed object can be a fid. A pin is a good fid. It is useful to keep a couple in the fly box or under a lapel. If the tangle is not drawn up too tight it can be unpicked with a fid. If the tangle was ignored, in the hope it would 'go away' (they never do), or yanked tight in exasperation, then cut your losses and tie on another piece of nylon.

Lines tangle around rod tips, branches, grass and other vegetation and itself. Line around rod tips is usually easily sorted. Branches are a problem. Alders in particular exert an attraction over flies and lines which often brings them into contact. If an alder reaches out and grabs your fly, despite your carefully judged back cast, stop. A gentle draw will sometimes retrieve flies, spinners and other tackle. If this doesn't work, go to the tree, remove the whole branch containing your tackle and then taking it apart twig by twig clear it from your line, do this in a clear area.

Do not pull at tangles using your rod; it doesn't work and it will ruin a split-cane rod. If you have to pull for a break as a last resort, rather than

On Knots and Tangles

leaving line in a tree remove the branch, with a saw if necessary. Leaving long lengths of nylon in trees is perhaps the worst thing an angler can do.

Bankside vegetation is surprisingly tough when hooked, even a blade of grass will put up a struggle. Again, you may have to wade across to take on the offending vegetation, cow parsley, nettle etc. It is the price to pay for fishing in Arcady.

Line tangling around line is frustrating, do not pull hard and hope, it doesn't work. A nylon tippet in a tangle is usually best cut off and replaced. Leaders, being thicker nylon, do not pull up so tight and are usually easily untangled. Fine nylon tippet tangled around flyline is tricky. Nylon will cut into flyline, so don't pull it, cut it away and tie on fresh. Any knot, kink or damage to nylon can weaken it so, if in doubt, replace tippets from the spare spool in your pocket. Waste nylon must be collected up; a small plastic container such as a film canister is ideal.

Knots are given names, so are tangles. Most are not fit for publication. The only two that I wish to write down here follow.

Firstly, the wind-knot. It is a simple tangle in the form of an over-hand or Granny knot. If it is not spotted and removed it can lead to the loss of a fish of a lifetime. It is often formed by tired casting or casting into the wind. Check your tippet and leader frequently as, if left, it reduces nylon to the strength of cotton.

The second named tangle is the 'Birds-nest', a much more serious affair. Commonly encountered by the bait angler who, ignoring a loose loop of line on a fixed-spool reel, casts out to find something that looks like a ball of scribble jammed into the rod rings.

As I say, tangles have many names, I will not sully these pages with them. No doubt you will be moved to find a few more. Fishing is a simple act, a rod, line, and hook, and a thousand ways of messing it up.

Avoiding tangles? Tangles like death and taxes come to all. The novice will no doubt meet with a tangle before his first fish. Novices, mistaking finches for fishes, send their flies into the branches where trout rarely venture.

On Knots and Tangles

Careful casting will avoid most wind-knots, but not all. The novice should keep his tackle simple. He, and the graduate from still-water, may benefit by restricting the number of flies on their wet-fly cast to a maximum of two. Fish with as stout nylon as you can. A mayfly on a fine tippet is a good source of tangles and a fairly stout tippet will make it much easier to retrieve flies from the vegetation.

The border angler may take a pair of secateurs in his back pocket. Not only will he be able to remove any branch that his fly seeks cover in but, by removing it, he will aid himself the next time he fishes there. Obviously, if you do not have permission to do this, refrain from removing anything larger than twigs. As well as secateurs a little fold-away pruning saw comes in useful. It is amazing how quickly and easily an impossible jungle can be made fishable.

Lastly, simply avoid the trees. Fish the open pools and the main river; don't make hard work for yourself. When you are ready, then go explore the jungle sections and small overgrown streams.

BORDER FLIES

This Welsh Border area has a rich history when it comes to fly patterns and styles, flies such as the Red Tag. It was first known as the Worcestershire Gem, and used for the grayling of the Tenbury area in 1850. Many other less well-known patterns originated in this area and are documented in several excellent books on the subject.

Border flies have a style different from chalk-stream patterns. Although most anglers fish with shop bought flies of standard construction, there was a tradition of constructing border flies to suit border conditions. Flies dressed in a standard manner, with a body on the hook shank and a hackle at the eye end of the hook, have been around for many years and from time to time dressers have experimented with reversing the hackle (to the bend end), tying on two hackles (either end), a hackle all the way along ('Palmered' hackle), or even turning the hackle so that lies flat on the water ('Parachute hackle'). Most of these have been in response to difficult fish where hiding the hook or producing a more realistic image of the fly was the aim; many of these originated from chalk-stream anglers.

Our border rivers present a different problem. In fast broken water floatation is key, and on heavily bushed streams where precise gentle casts are difficult, the first priority of the dry fly is that it should float. Various methods have been used to achieve this. The multiple hackle styles are all represented and a series of reverse hackle flies were popular, not only for their realistic and floating qualities, but also that they were less likely to become attached to branches due to the hackle guarding the hook point. Now they are rarely seen for sale, and seem to have lost their popularity.

Unfortunately for those fishing border-waters any well hackled fly, especially with hackles that cover the hook point, can impede hooking the fish. A fly bristling with stiff hackles gives the fish, especially grayling, the opportunity to push it aside with its snout or to reject it as soon as it feels any resistance.

A problem with conventionally dressed patterns on rough border waters is that they get waterlogged and sink, or at least the rear section does. If the angler increases the tail with stiff material there is a danger it will reduce hooking ability. The angler still sees the floating fly, but often with only the hackles above water, the rest awash, sunk tail first. Most emerger patterns feature a submerged or semi-submerged body. They are increasingly popular on border streams and effective fish takers. Hackle, hair or some other buoyant material is tied in at the eye to form a thorax, while the body is intended to be fished awash. Examples are the Neen Nymph and the Klinkhammer. On border streams this makes a virtue out of the problem of waterlogged bodies.

For steadier flows the parachute hackle works well; it puts the hackle flat and level with the water where it can support the fly, the body floats on the surface, as the natural, and a wing post adds visibility.

For turbulent water and situations where the reverse hackle was seen as a solution in the past, the angler could follow the American enthusiasm for deer hair and use a Deer Hair Sedge, or a Compara Dun pattern or, alternatively, a fly dressed with CDC such as the Little Hereford. Various patterns are commercially available and there is little difficulty in dressing a dozen or so of various sizes.

There is a longstanding topic of discussion between anglers: the importance of imitation over presentation.

One argues that the trout will take an imitation that is approximately the same size, shape and colour as the natural, as long as presentation is entirely natural. The other states that the trout will refuse a fly that differs from the natural and so presentation is irrelevant. Yet another would say that presentation is part of imitation and, why wouldn't you want to present the best possible imitation in the best possible way?

As with many other fly-fishing debates, it centres on chalk-stream fishing. How does the argument effect our swift little border rivers where the hungry trout are less fussy?

Chalk-stream trout enjoy clear water flowing at a steady unbroken pace; they have more time to view their food. Chalk-streams traditionally produce big hatches of single species, and their trout focus on these ignoring other flies appearing in small numbers, they become 'selective' trout. The Chalk-stream angler closely matched these hatches, while the country folk of Shropshire dressed patterns from materials that were to hand that had the look and attitude of the natural. Chalk-streams are fished far more than border streams, most days there will be an angler on that beat, they become wary of a badly presented fly, labelled 'educated' trout.

The novice would do well to choose a fly of similar colour, size and attitude to those seen on the water. Selecting a fly because someone caught a fish on a What's 'is name's Wonder, or Somebodies Fancy, is simply handing it over to chance.

Some stretches of the Teme are not fished in a year, and a trout may never see an angler's fly. Hatches are very varied and usually border trout will take anything that looks like food floating over them. The various subtle differences between species is of academic rather than practical interest. Presentation would seem to be simple, but chalk-streams are generally not heavily over grown, so there is a similar element of difficulty. Whereas on chalk-streams many patterns have developed to imitate a few natural flies, on border streams patterns are more all-purpose. Many chalk-stream patterns work on border rivers with minor modifications. Traditionalists may enjoy using the established patterns.

Border fly hatches are quite simple and a few flies cover most occasions. Our trout usually take a fly that is similar in size, shape, colour, and posture on the water as the natural. An imitation, dressed with regard to these criteria, is as likely to succeed as the best shop bought fly.

If you dress your own flies (parcels are tied, flies are dressed) then a whole new world of opportunity is open to you. You can imitate the particular flies on your river in their correct sizes, colours and posture as you observe them on the river. It is a great advantage to have the fly you need, in the size you need, and in the numbers you need, given that a few of them are bound to disappear into the trees. If you do not dress your own it is more difficult, and expensive to have a good selection of suitable flies in various sizes.

Fly-dressing

It is not necessary to be able to dress flies to be able to catch trout, in the same way that you don't need to be able to cook, to eat, but it helps. As with food and cooking it gives much greater choice, not only in fly patterns but importantly in sizes. The fly is the most important part of the angler's tackle and the only part the trout should see. The angler with a well stocked fly box will certainly be at an advantage.

However much is spent on rods, reels, lines, or the day's fishing, it all comes to nothing if the trout will not take the fly. As a novice I was apprehensive about using home-made flies. Shop bought flies were 'correct' and my attempts were scruffy looking and I had no confidence in them. Trial and error soon showed the trout have no respect for 'correct' flies, in fact I'm sure I heard them snigger when a shop bought size fourteen 'Iron Blue' floated over their heads. Time on the water revealed that 'iron blues' (*Baetis niger*) are about a size eighteen and dark grey, not blue. Success came, and confidence followed. As the angler and writer Datus Proper said, listen to the trout, the trout will tell you what is correct.

Fly-dressing at its simplest is covering the hook so as to imitate something the trout will eat. It is a skill and like all skills it takes a little time to gain, but once gained it adds another layer of pleasure and insight to your angling. The basic skills will ensure that it doesn't unwrap, beyond that there are no rules.

There are recipes for certain patterns, some of them work, but many traditional patterns ask for materials that are difficult, expensive or even impossible to obtain. There is nothing to stop anyone using an alternative material and, if it matches the fly on the water, it might improve it.

Beware of simply following complex patterns for no good reason. The fly is a means to an end, not the end itself. Dozens of patterns fill monthly magazines recommended by fishermen who have caught a few fish on it, sometimes their friend caught fish on it as well.

Richard Walker, an angler who knew a thing or two, said that you should catch fifty fish on a fly before publicising it, and even then, I would suggest giving it to friends to get their opinion too. Don't follow the crowd, your attempt can be just as effective as that in the glossy magazine. We dress flies to impress trout not anglers.

Style

A fly that looks 'right' will inspire confidence and will be fished more effectively. We aim to catch beautiful fish with beautiful flies. If you dress any fly you are not satisfied with it is better you clean it off the hook and start again; you will not use it, it will sit in your fly box as an embarrassment.

To look right, and importantly to fish right, the fly must have the right proportions. It must do the things intended, that is a dry fly must float, wet flies must sink. The most common fault when starting fly-dressing is to 'over dress' and cram too much dressing on the fly, let your motto be 'less is more'.

Always, wet or dry, leave the body of the fly short of the bend of the hook. Specialist patterns may call for a curved body carried around the bend, but apart from specific patterns, keep bodies short.

Hackles should just come to the hook point with a wet-fly, while dry fly hackles should stand the fly on any surface so the hackle points, hook bend and tail act as the three points of contact. Then it will not only look correct, it will have the correct balance.

Another area where balance is important is colour. Look at natural flies when deciding on a fishing fly; follow the colour of the natural when picking an artificial from the box.

When dressing flies use harmonious colours, checked in daylight, throughout. Few flies have green bodies and red legs; most green or olive coloured flies contain shades of yellow or grey. Flies predominantly red will shade to rusty brown.

Use silks of a base colour such as red or yellow and blend in materials that follow the tone or hue. Use of natural materials will help here. They show subtle shades and infinite variations and their fine graduations in size make a delicate fly. Similar to the charm of cane rods, the use of natural materials in fly-dressing has its devotees.

While anglers strive to replicate the colour of the natural insect there are some flies dressed, mainly those aimed at grayling, which have a more fanciful palette. Black is always good for a start; a touch of red, not too much; russet and gold, for the leaves of autumn; green ofttimes works, apple green to reflect the orchards along the banks, and a twist of silver for the sparkle of the stream.

Fly Patterns

For a novice fly-dresser it must be bewildering following the latest patterns. New patterns are advertised each month in magazines, each competing for a place in the fly box. These magazines need to fill their pages and fly patterns fill the space. Unfortunately for the beginner there is a baffling number of flies, most of which will only last in popularity until the next issue.

There is a similarity between cooking and fly-dressing. Both use recipes, both use ingredients, and both need a careful mix to achieve a good result. A famous chef said that many great recipes start with the same basic ingredients; in fly-dressing this could be 'tie in some well waxed yellow thread'. Yellow cotton thread when waxed with cobbler's wax turns a dirty brown, which when whipped around a hook shank, gives a wonderful segmented olive, sufficient to be a body on its own, as in the Greenwell's Glory. Add a wisp of hare's ear to the waxy thread and use that to form a tapered body and you are on the way to a classic; tie in a little gold wire or tinsel and wind that over the top and you have that classic dish, the Gold Ribbed Hare's Ear, one of the top flies of all time. Add a hackle of speckled feather taken from a game bird's wing and you have a March Hare. Leave out the hackle and tie in a good tuft of CDC and you have, well I don't know what to call it, an 'F' Fly, a Duck's Dun without hackle, whatever, it is another good simple fly from a basic recipe. Let's call it a Little Hereford because it also appears in the book.

All these flies work and work well, they may not be 'proper' patterns like those in the magazines but, like a classic steak, they are good because they come from good ingredients and no messing. The novice adds materials to a fly to make it attractive, experience teaches to leave stuff out: less is more.

While on the subject of ingredients, it is inevitable that the novice will collect more materials than he will use, thanks in part to the aforesaid magazines who come up with a new wonder material every other week: ignore them. Also ignore those patterns that call for obscure materials that are very expensive or hard to find. To dress a Greenwell's Glory correctly a particular patterned hackle is required, a good example is hard to find. Similarly the Tup's Indispensable uses a rarely found hackle, and singular body material. Most patterns offered use substitutes, they are variants, sometimes it is not easy to detect anything of the original, but the variants still work. Better still to use what is available cheaply and dress your flies to imitate the natural, not the picture in a magazine. Listen to the trout, the trout will tell you if it's a good fly, he'll eat it.

A final thought. You may find trout continue to take a certain fly even when it has been reduced to shreds. They still rise even to a wisp of dressing. What then do the trout take it for? Is it still the same pattern as when it was tied on? Is there something special in the dressing that is causing the reaction? So many questions remain to be answered. It shows that a fly does not need to be beautifully dressed and pristine, a scruffy, skinny fly is often successful.

Natural Flies

Historically it was thought there were only a few species of fly. At the start of the year there were the spring olives, these became lighter in colour and smaller in size as the warmth increased, until in summer they were palest and smallest. Then, as Autumn took hold, the flies became larger and darker.

Of course, there were exceptions to this. On cold wet days little iron blues appeared alongside larger spring olives and special flies such as the large Mayfly appear in warm weather; nevertheless, the idea has merit. Today we would say there are many species, but it matters little on the stream so long as the imitation is a match for the natural. So many patterns have been devised to imitate just one natural fly, such as the blue-winged olive or a spring olive, that it is impossible to say what the trout takes it for.

The small-stream angler has an advantage. He is often wading, he is able to bend down and lift the hatching fly or the spinner from the water and compare it with his artificial. He sees the mayfly nymph upbreaking the surface and struggling to get out of its nymphal case. He is even able to lift it out and have it emerge on the hand, a minor miracle. All fly life and trout food floating by, on or in, the surface can be examined close up. It is small scale, intimate, and immediate.

Nymphs

On border waters nymphs vary little in overall form or colour, with the exception of the mayfly. Underwater samples taken from the river bed show that most of the food available is very small, size 16 or less, and with few exceptions most of what trout eat is drab or dun coloured, hence the adage to 'try something small and dark'. A few artificial nymphs in sizes 14 and 16 in olive or natural coloured pheasant tail should cover most of the needs of border anglers.

Weight and loading are the key with nymph dressing. Nymphs with beads, such as an Option 2, fish deep in the bottom layer, unweighted nymphs, or dressings that include fur or hackle, fish higher in the water and in the surface film.

Dressing Your Own Patterns

If an angler is able to dress his own flies, it is likely that he will adapt a pattern, a variant of an established fly, to suit his home streams. It may be as simple as a few more turns of hackle to aid floatation on rougher stretches, or a change of materials to better represent the insect he finds on the water.

Some patterns may be changed past all recognition. They are beyond a variant: they become a new pattern. Fly-dressers experiment with new patterns all the time, most work quite well, few work consistently, and even fewer work consistently over time.

Included here are a few personally named patterns. Firstly, they are included because they feature in the text of the tales by the river bank, and it becomes bothersome to continually write, 'a small nymph similar to...' or 'but with a hackle of...'. So the flies have names rather than descriptions, for brevity and clarity.

Secondly, personal experience and trial by others has proved their effectiveness. Therefore, if any angler might profit, they are welcome.

Neen Nymph

This simple pattern can be fished as a nymph or an emerging dun. It is a Hare's Ear Emerger Nymph, abbreviated to H.E.E.N. for the diary to distinguish it from a Hare's Ear Nymph. Over time Heen Nymph became Neen Nymph, after the villages through which the river Rea flows, Neenton, Neen Savage, and Neen Sollars.

The pattern is basic and no doubt has been used many times before, but, as a recognised name for it couldn't be found, one was invented.

Take a size sixteen hook medium weight, a curved or straight shank is fine. Thread is orange for Blue-winged olive imitations, or well waxed yellow for general Olives. Does it make any difference? Probably not, but it gives confidence. Run the tread to the end of the shank and tie in some fine copper wire. Tie in some pheasant tail, leaving a short tail, wrap the pheasant tail two thirds of the way up the shank forming a short, tapered body and tie in. Rib with the wire. Dub the thread with hare's ear and form a thick thorax/upper body. Tie off.

To fish, if it is greased it will float, if soaked it will sink. If you spit on the tail end or rub with mud, while picking out and lightly greasing the hare's ear, it will float with the tail dipped in the water rather like an emerging olive. It can be deadly for grayling in the autumn.

The Burford Red

The Burford Red was conceived as a wet-fly to be fished downstream, primarily for grayling. It is designed to sink first time, every time, and to swim at sufficient depth below the surface so as not to skate, or cause a wake.

The fly needs to be small but to have a good silhouette, a thorax, a slim body, and a fairly dense mobile hackle. This hackle has to be soft so, that when drawn through the water, it will fold and enclose, or encapsulate the fly's body to give a streamlined nymph-like outline. The hackle should also veil the body to give an image of translucency. The body is fine bright red wire, not copper, but red. This is muted by the hackle veiling and gives the illusion of a deeper, copper tone. The head, hackle, and thread are black, this gives a good outline or silhouette and a good contrast to the red body so, despite its small size, it is readily seen in the rough water. There is a small thorax of peacock herl, to give a dark iridescent bulk to the thorax and to reinforce the bulk of the hackle; the hackle being wound on top of the herl, not in front or behind. This gives a small neat thorax tapering to the slim body, a characteristic of a swimming nymph.

Movement is a trigger. Food moves: what moves is food. A mobile hackle is important, not only to give shape but also to give a flickering veil over the bright body. Lastly, the hackle should move independently in the current, similar to a soft hackle spider pattern fly.

The red body is a conspicuous colour that is a trigger for trout and grayling, their eyes picking up the red end of the spectrum better than the blue. How many good blue trout flies are there?

The materials are cheap and easy to obtain. Mount the hook. A medium weight size sixteen with a wide gape is ideal; a size fourteen dressed short is fine. Run black thread down the shank and tie in the thin bright red wire then wind a neat, even, tapering body to two thirds of the way to the eye.

The wire may not lie exactly in tight touching turns, but the slight gap will show through as banding, so that's fine.

Tie off the wire and tie in the black hackle and a thin rope of three bronze peacock herls twisted together. A couple of turns of the herl will form a small thorax. Tie off and wind the hackle on top of the herl, use a soft, full, webby hackle, a couple of turns will do. The length of the hackle should be enough to enclose the body, but no more. Too much hackle and it will not collapse. Tie off to give a slight backward sweep to the hackle. It is a simple fly but one where the details make the difference.

Tails or tags on grayling flies are problematic. An experienced local angler told me he believed grayling take flies by nipping at the tail. Richard Walker held that trigger points, like tags, could work better by improving hooking if moved further up the fly, as in his Sweeny Todd fly, which has red at the throat. The Burford Red has no tail, the red body being the trigger.

This year the Burford Red has been my most successful pattern for grayling, but it also was responsible for two dozen trout.

When trout fishing it is usually employed in those situations when a trout is rising, or at least moving, to feed at the surface but can't be tempted with a dry fly. A Burford Red is cast upstream to land just ahead of the fish, the fly will land quite softly due to the hackle (unlike a weighted nymph) and will slowly sink just below the surface. No doubt trout take it for a terrestrial insect that has fallen in, and not only trout but also Teme chub and roach and even still-water rainbow trout have fallen for this dodge.

The Option 2

This is another pattern that has been adapted from a standard, in this case a Pheasant Tail Nymph. It used to be noted in the diary as, Olive Pheasant Tail Nymph 2 beads. Then a short step from O.P.T.N.2. to Option 2.

So what are the changes from a Pheasant Tail Nymph? The Pheasant Tail Nymph was famously made from natural pheasant tail and red copper wire. The Option 2 has none of that.

To start put in the vice a medium weight size sixteen hook with a fairly long shank. Not a Long Shank hook but you will need a fairly long shank to work on. Using fine black thread, tie in a thin strip of dark olive-green plastic at the eye, tag end facing back down the shank, this will form a thorax cover over the two beads. Ensure that the tag end is neatly tied in and whip finish. Then thread the two black 2mm tungsten beads on, they should fit tightly up against the hook eye, if the tag has been neatly tied in. Tie in some black thread just behind the beads and use it to bind down the plastic thorax cover tightly, so that the beads are held firmly in place. Cut off the plastic strip and run the thread down to the end of the shank. Tie in some pheasant tail, dyed dark olive green. Tie in some fine gold wire. Leaving a short tail, wind the pheasant tail up to form a tapered body, rib with the gold wire and tie off tight behind the beads.

The effect should be that of a slim Pheasant Tail Nymph with a dark thorax. The beads are small but heavy and included within the dressing. The whole thing should be streamlined.

It is very useful fished singly upstream where a deep nymph is needed to reach the bottom when trout are reluctant to feed at higher levels. It will sink quickly and be small enough to closely imitate an Olive nymph; otherwise it is very effective fished downstream as the tail fly of a team of wet flies to anchor and steady the cast. A good dropper fly in this case would be a Burford Red.

A companion to the Neen Nymph, which imitates the olive dun freshly hatched, or emerging; the Option 2 is a deeper fishing nymph covering all levels on the river. If you have a few of each in your fly box, you will never be without an option.

Red Spinner

This is a fly that has many dressings but this is the one described in the book so it is included here, although you may prefer your own choice.

Border Flies

Start with a size sixteen lightweight hook, a size eighteen with a slightly longer shank is also good.

The silk or thread is hot orange which, when well waxed with cobbler's wax, turns a lovely deep chestnut.

The tail is a few red cock hackle fibres, quite long, at least the same length as the body.

The body, pheasant tail herl. Dyed claret, or better still if you can find it, a tail feather of a natural deep rich chestnut red.

A rib of finest gold is all that is needed, or none at all.

Wings should not be over long lest they loop under the bend of the hook. They can be a blue grey hackle tied in and then split with a figure of eight binding to produce two horizontal wings. Alternatively use waterproof yarn, or even blue-grey hackle tips.

Hackle tips look nice but are fiddly to tie and prone to spin the fly like a propeller. The way to avoid the problem is to wind a hackle in front of the wings, to break up the air flow.

To complete, a short sparse hackle of natural red cock is wound over and in front of the wing. Smaller sizes need not have a hackle.

A spot of varnish on the head will secure the thread and make the orange silk glow.

The Suir Thing

The next fly comes with a story, of a fishing holiday in Ireland on the River Suir. My host on the river presented me with a parachute style fly which he said was the only one I would ever need, and very effective it was too. Wherever I cast, I rose a trout. These trout were mostly around eight inches long with the best, a ten inch monster. My host was delighted at the constant action which he declared the finest fishing in the world. One thing puzzled me, how to pronounce 'Suir'. We finally came to agreement on it sounding like 'sure' and so the 'Suir Thing' was christened.

Place a medium weight size sixteen hook in the vice, and start some well waxed yellow thread at the eye and run it down half-way down the shank.

Tie in some white calf tail to make a wing post and lift upright.

Continue the thread down to the end of the shank and tie in a tail of grizzle cock fibres.

Wax the thread and dub very lightly with blue rabbit fur. Wind up forming a tapered body, until reaching the wing post.

Tie in a short fibred grizzle hackle, wind on parachute style and tie off.

Dub the thread with more blue rabbit and finish off the thorax. Whip finish at the eye.

Black Gnat

The classic 'little black fly', simple to dress and a good fly for the novice to practice on. Try to get it in perfect proportion; not even the 'experts' can always do that.

Start with a medium weight size sixteen hook and tie in a short cock hackle, continue a bed of black thread to the rear of the hook.

Tie in a short tail (optional) of cock hackle and a body of dyed black herl, omit the tail and herl on small sizes (18 & 20) or when using as a wet-fly.

When the body is wound back to the head, wind the hackle and tie off.

For a very effective wet-fly simply tie in a soft hen hackle and use the black thread as a body, silver rib is optional.

Dressed with a little wing of white yarn or feather fibre it stands out on dark water.

For an effective Hawthorn Fly pattern, dress it on a size fourteen or even size twelve hook. Then you can add two knotted black pheasant tail legs, if that is your fancy.

The March Hare

The March Hare is nothing particularly new or different, it is included for two reasons. Firstly, it is mentioned in the book and it should be described. Secondly, it shows a wet-fly pattern that is easy to dress for a beginner, uses simple materials and works well.

The March Brown, which is similar, is a good wet-fly, but the natural which it imitates is rare on the Teme. It is so rare that the trout probably take the artificial for a Spring or Large Dark Olive. My diary shows that on the last day of April the March Hare fished downstream took five trout in an hour during a hatch of Spring Olives. The March Hare is a humble imitation of an olive, but also would serve in a larger size for a March Brown, should you be lucky enough to be on the water when there is a hatch.

In the early days of autumn the Teme grayling lie in the faster flows, in the fast, shallow fords. Then, when they are taking freely, it is enjoyable and profitable to fish a March Hare to them in traditional wet-fly style.

Start with a size fourteen hook, medium or heavy weight. Tie in some well waxed yellow thread at the head and run it half way down.

Tie in a small short tail of a mottled game-bird feather, such as grouse, woodcock or partridge.

Stop the thread short of the bend and dub on a thin wisp of pale hare's ear. A rib of gold wire or very fine tinsel is optional.

The body is wound back up to form a taper and another game bird feather, as above, tied in by the tip and wound two or three times. Form a small head and tie off.

Nothing new, it looks a little like a wingless March Brown, or it could be a skinny Gold Ribbed Hare's Ear with a hackle. It doesn't matter, it is simple to dress, uses easily found materials, and it works.

To fish, as the name suggests, it is a good wet-fly for early season. When little is rising, a trout can often be brought to a March Hare fished wet downstream. Cast across and allowed to fish dead drift like an olive emerging, the soft hackle moving in the current may provoke a rise. As it sinks and drifts downstream, work it around and it will rise up in the current, the soft hackle folding back over the body and flickering in the current giving the impression of a nymph swimming to the surface. Fished upstream, on or just below the surface, it has deceived many difficult fish.

Gold Ribbed Hare's Ear

This is a much-copied fly and many variations are to be found. The original used nothing more than well waxed thread, hare's ear, and gold wire. Today you will see it with wings, hackles and goodness knows what else. With the motto 'less is more' here is a dressing using the original three ingredients.

First, for ease, simply tie in well-waxed thread, cobbler's wax on cotton thread works well, and run the thread to the bend.

Tie in a fine gold-wire rib.

The hare's ear is dubbed on the thread, very thinly at first then thicker to form a taper. Fine, pale fur for the body and coarser darker hair at the thorax adds realism.

Wind the ribbing up the body and tie off.

Finally, pick out the thorax and 'hackle' with a pin or Velcro pad.

Next, for dressers who want a little test of dexterity, try this.

Set a size fourteen or sixteen medium-weight hook in the vice. Run well-waxed yellow thread to the rear of the shank.

Select a small bunch of hare's mask fur, as long and straight as possible, clean it to remove all fluff and under fur, and tie in as a tail.

Tie in fine gold wire or very fine tinsel.

Using the soft under-fur from the hare's mask, lightly dub the thread with a wisp of fur and form a fine tapered body.

Rib with wire or tinsel.

Now, using the same procedure as the tail, select and clean a good bunch of long and straight hare's mask fibres, these will make the hackle. When they are completely clean of fluff lay them carefully to one side on your working surface where they can be picked up later.

The thread that was hanging must now be doubled or split. To split insert a dubbing needle or similar into the thread to separate and then spin the thread so that the needle can be brought towards you as it untwists, insert your finger to keep it open. If your thread is fine try doubling it over the hook shank to give a large loop facing you. Hold it taut with the hook end of a whip- finish tool, baiting hook or what have you. Hold the strands open with your finger.

Now the tricky part, transfer the prepared fibres to sit midway between the split thread or in the loop. Damp fingers or a dab of spit helps. Try to get no more than an inch or three centimetres spread of fibre by positioning in the split and by carefully drawing in the loop.

Keeping it tight, spin the thread, in both cases, to trap the fibres. The fibres will flare out (a few may fall out, if they all fall out you may flare instead). It takes practice.

What you have now can be wound around the shank; like pancakes, the first one rarely works. Once wound, the fibres can be preened and forced into place to give a good collar 'hackle'.

Some of your swans may turn out to be geese: then after a while, dry flies the equivalent of cock hackled examples can be dressed.

They are excellent takers of trout. Early season trout taking spring olives will especially fall for them. Just don't lose too many in the trees!

And a few tips

Any fly will benefit from having a thin layer of varnish spread on the hook shank before the thread is whipped on. The varnish soaks into the thread and strengthens the fly: a thin coat on the hook first will make it last. This precaution also helps stop the dressing slipping back on the hook and causing bad language.

As flies get bedraggled and (hopefully) covered in slime, they no longer float. Ousted to a corner reserved for flies no longer fit for work, they languish. They need steaming. Wash off the worst of the mud, slime and whatever, then hold them with a pair of tweezers in the steam from the spout of a boiling kettle. Preened and teased back into shape they will be renewed, ready to take their place in the fly-box again.

The novice, and some experienced fly-dressers, should pay attention to ensure they finish the fly short of the hook eye. Too close and the dressing obstructs the eye and makes threading the fly onto the line a difficult task; sealing the eye with varnish makes it impossible.

Hooks

Hooks for fly-dressing come in a confusing number of styles and weights. Choose barbless, of course, you may lose a few fish off barbless hooks, but no more than on barbed, and barbless hooks are so much easier to remove from fish, your jumper, or your finger.

As for size, if you kick sample the Teme or any local stream you will find nearly everything that trout eat is equivalent to a hook size sixteen or less.

The exceptions are mayfly and some sedge, start with size sixteen for dry flies, and size fourteen wet flies dressed short.

Dressing 'short' basically means stopping short along the shank, short of the bend, also called 'tying within the hook' meaning the dressing is restrained and the hackle is kept within the gape of the hook.

Limiting the dressing on a wet-fly enables it to sink quickly, and using a hook one size larger is reasonable. Restraint in use of materials is an important lesson for the novice.

To start, keep it simple. A normal straight shank hook will cover most needs and medium weight will work in most situations. Avoid very lightweight hooks. They work for very minimalist skinny patterns, perhaps spinners fished on a very fine tippet on a windless summers evening, but they can be a bother in normal fishing. The problem is that a little weight is desirable to turn over the leader, especially when casting in awkward corners and tight spots, so medium weight is the way to go.

A good friend and very fine fly-fisher told me that he and his brother bought silver hooks one time and dressed flies on them, they couldn't raise a fish. I noticed the same thing, lack of confidence? Possibly, personal choice is for dark colours for hooks and no flash.

Finally, a detail for thought. Trout and salmon, and possibly some coarse fish, have the ability to navigate by using the earth's magnetic field. They are very sensitive to magnetic influences. Some hooks are strongly magnetic. Some fly boxes hold flies by magnetic strips. Whether this puts off trout rising to the fly is debateable and, like many things in angling, difficult to prove until we find a trout that will talk to us. Perhaps it is more relevant to the bait fisher whose hook lies on the bottom where fish approach and examine it at leisure, than the strike of a trout, but it is a detail. Should the carp fisher waiting hours, even days, for a carp to take, have ensured the hook wasn't magnetic? One more thing for him to think about. To demagnetise a hook is simple. The process is called 'degauss' and a little device costing a few pounds is used, the hooks being drawn through to remove the magnetism. It is worth thinking about.

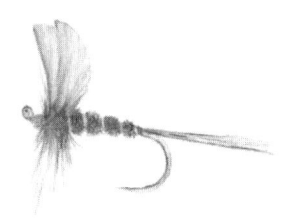

ON DRESS

Here are some thoughts on clothing suitable for fishing our border streams. Emphasis should be on comfort and practicality.

On border streams you will rarely drive up to the fishing and saunter along a short, level path to the water's edge as you may do on a still-water.

Border anglers have a need for items that are tough and flexible. Clothes must allow the angler to climb up and down steep banks.

They must keep him warm when wading in cool water and cool on a long hot walk across rough ground. If at all possible, they should be cheap.

Starting at the head. A hat of your choice gives an opportunity for expression of sartorial individuality. In the hot sun it provides shade and, in the cold, keeps you warm. On border streams it will give some protection from twigs and nettles. It will also give you something, other than your skin, to douse with insect repellent. Moreover its shade will enhance your vision, rather like cupping your hands around your eyes.

On Dress

Those who shoot will tell you that a hat will help conceal your face, an obvious mark against the shadows of the river bank, and useful if you are well-known to the trout.

In the evening a broad brim, or peak will cut out the dazzling rays of the setting sun. Finally, you can stick flies in it, if you are so inclined.

A jacket is the next item. We are fortunate in Britain to have developed a good tool for this job, the sports jacket. Called a sports jacket because it was designed to be worn when hunting, shooting and fishing. The vents cut into the back allow it to fall over the back of a saddle, an addition of bellows vents allows the shooter to mount and swing his gun. The lapels button across, using the button hole, to protect the wearer in extreme cold or driving rain.

Made from wool, a stout jacket is breathable and waterproof. Its traditional colours were chosen to mimic the surrounding countryside. The Victorian sportsman chose his palette to merge with his surroundings.

A good jacket of tweed cloth in a check pattern will consist of earthy browns and greens, with a touch of purple heather or yellow gorse. It may be whimsical to suggest that a good jacket worn with a certain panache may evoke a rise from an otherwise reluctant trout, but it can't hurt.

A sports jacket for a border angler is a practical item of clothing with practical pockets that hold practically all he needs for an evening on the river. If warm from a long walk across the fields it can be unbuttoned and on hot days, hung from a branch. Perhaps best of all it can be obtained for just a few pounds from a second-hand clothing shop. It may be a little marked or frayed but then fishing jackets should be.

Such a jacket is not a nostalgic, sentimental longing for the past, it is recognition that fitting, well-worn and appropriate things still have a place. A jacket and tie are still practical, and the sports jacket, along with the wellington boot, is one of the great advances in civilisation.

A cotton shirt can be worn under a jacket. Darker, earthy colours will blend in with the vegetation of overgrown streams. On the chill days of spring, the addition of a woollen tie will keep your neck warm. On hot days temperature control is by buttons. On very hot days the jacket can be discarded and a shirt with two good sized breast pockets will suffice with a fly box, note pad, pencil and tape in one and a couple of spools of nylon in the other. Some excellent olive-coloured shirts are available from army surplus market stalls.

Whenever possible wear a long-sleeved shirt or jacket. The banks of the Teme have some of the country's finest nettle beds. Few border river banks have no stinging nettles and even a small nettle sting is painful and a lasting irritation. For similar reasons shorts are rarely a good idea.

On cold days a cravat or stock in the form of a strip of olive-green 'netting' or towelling as worn by wildfowlers is a boon, keeping your neck snug and warm. In a heavy shower it will stop the rain trickling down your neck.

Waders cover the clothing of most anglers below the waist. Waders are chosen with regard to the water being fished, either chestwaders or thighwaders. On border streams as you will be walking a fair distance and climbing up and down steep banks, a pair of breathable chestwaders are a good investment. They may be economy, entry-level, budget or whatever but they are much more comfortable than non-breathable and being too hot will ruin your day as surely as being too cold.

Chestwaders usually rely on a wading boot, again there is little need to go for the most expensive pair for border streams. As for soles, plain ridged rubber is a little slippery in-stream and when climbing out up steep banks.

Felt soles work well on slippery, slime covered summer-time rocks, but not so well on banks. Felt soles with studs on the heels, or in combination, work on both.

Be aware that felt soles can transfer disease and organisms and may not be welcome everywhere. Newer sticky rubber soles with small studs are a good alternative. As always, if wading in faster, deeper water, or wherever you feel unsafe, wear an automatic buoyancy aid.

Waders wear out after a season or two, so ensure you know how to make basic repairs which extend their life. Old, worn waders can be used for bank-work in the closed-season.

If you only fish waters where thighwaders are needed, then ensure you always have a belt. Most,

On Dress

if not all, thighwaders hang from one. The absence of a belt may entail borrowing some bailer twine to stop them falling down.

ON ACCESSORIES

The main items of tackle needed to fish border waters have been discussed in previous chapters. From rod and reel through lines, leaders, tippets to flies and even what to wear, all have been considered. Now it is time to deal with those things not directly involved in catching a fish, but are nevertheless important to success or comfort and are particularly suited to our needs on border streams, and consider if others are necessary.

Those going on an extended trip, or of a forgetful nature, may wish to make a list, an aide-memoire to ensure all necessary things are taken (and to highlight those which are never used).

Fly-fishing tackle is assessed first, with a few bait fishing suggestions given towards the end. Imagine you are at the waterside and have all the tackle made up in the form of a fly rod and reel, line leader and tippet in hand. The next thing is to tie on a fly.

So firstly, the fly box. For ease and simplicity try to manage with just one fly box on the river. If

On Accessories

you really feel the need for more, take them with you and leave them in the car. At home you will have a store of flies from which you can fill your fly box with those that are needed. If only the relevant flies are chosen, it is rare to need more than a moderately sized box.

At mayfly time a special mayfly box is brought along, similarly in early spring or at grayling time a selection of wet flies or nymphs can be made up.

Always put different boxes in different pockets, otherwise you will be forever pulling out the wrong box. If they must go into the same pocket, ensure they can be told apart at a touch.

A fly box should be moderate in size to slip easily into the pocket, and ideally have separate compartments for dry flies and some foam for a few wet flies and nymphs. A fly box with a clear lid will show, at a glance, you have no more of your favourite fly. This is an important point, you will run out of your preferred flies first. Your favourite flies will be used more often, they will be lost in trees and shredded by trout. Renew them from your stores at home. Flies never used, and those that remain at the end of the season should be removed.

Consult your note book or diary (coming up) and those flies that caught fish, dress by the dozen; those unused, discard.

Scissors or clippers are needed, now the fly is tied on, to cut the tail ends of the knot. Nail clippers work well and don't stick into you as you climb banks as scissors may, no need to spend a lot on them. I have clippers from a Christmas cracker that work perfectly well and are kept in reserve in the car. An even better device is scissor pliers, a short pair of scissors with the tips flattened to act as lightweight pliers, just enough to be able to remove any awkward hooks. These can be attached to a retractable cord ('zinger') to hang discretely, but handily, from the lapel of your sports jacket.

However, suppose the fly selected had the eye covered with varnish or was blocked by a fly-dresser who hadn't read the advice in the section, 'On Border Flies', and had allowed the thread to cover the eye. In that case go for your fid. (Fid? – You really haven't been paying attention, see section, 'On Knots and Tangles). A fid, a knot unpicker, such as a pin can also be used to clear hook eyes. So add a couple of pins under the lapel of your jacket, and another in the fly box.

If the fly has come back waterlogged some means of drying it will be needed. Amadou can be used, but it is expensive and can be ruined if the grease from the fly gets onto it. Almost as good is strong kitchen roll, any strengthened paper product will do, as will a cotton handkerchief, or in extremis, the front of your cotton shirt.

Now the fly will need to be waterproofed. Anglers have their favourite products to use and most will work most of the time. Avoid anything that leaves an 'oil slick' on the water when the fly lands. Tubs of 'Red Mucilin' work and are inexpensive, smear just a little on your finger and warm it between finger and thumb, then work it onto the fly, it also works on nylon line if your leader starts to sink. I believe it is a natural animal grease or fat. Store it flat in a hot car or it will melt and waterproof your pocket.

Alternatively, you may want to sink your line and/or fly. The line can be run through clean kitchen paper or a dock leaf to remove grease. Then run through mud or clay from the bank to remove any remaining traces and encourage it to sink.

To sink flies, dip them in water or mud and roll them between finger and thumb. Some anglers spit on flies for luck, which is not a bad idea. Those crafty carp fishermen, who research into almost everything, tested various substances including human saliva, and found it to be an attractant. If you are wading mid-stream and cannot reach any mud, or even the damp moss from an alder root, nor a passing floating leaf, then some form of sinkant in your pocket is needed. Commercial products are available. Made at home it is simply fullers earth and glycerine or washing up liquid. Given the difficulty of obtaining fullers earth and the small amounts used it may be easier and cheaper to buy a ready made tub.

A fly patch or pad is needed on which flies that have been removed can be placed to dry out before being replaced in the fly box or reused when next needed. If stuck straight into your lapel, barbed hooks are a devil to remove, and barbless hooks will drop out. A serviceable fly patch can be made from a name badge to which has been glued closed cell foam. The patch is attached to the lapel of your jacket.

Tippet material is going to be needed as flies are changed and lost. Tippet lengths vary with the situation but eventually it becomes too short and is replaced. Slip the discarded nylon into a little plastic wallet or similar. Usually two spare spools of nylon of different thicknesses are sufficient.

A basic lightweight 'first aid' kit can be assembled from a couple of painkillers in a blister strip, a couple of waterproof plasters, and a couple of safety pins, all slipped into a 35mm film canister which will sit in the top pocket and be just enough to deal with minor cuts and headaches that may otherwise mar your day.

Licences and permits as needed can be slipped into the top pocket and be at hand if required.

A note book or pad with a couple of pencil stubs, sharpened at both ends in case one loses its point, and a cheap dress-makers tape cut down for convenience to 20" or 24" (depends on your confidence), will record each fish. Some may feel that is over zealous, indeed it may be, it does, however, ensure no fish is forgotten. Also, it shows respect for the fish and guards against inflated stories.

The small note pad, of the style used by policemen, is useful not only for recording fish caught, but also for recording thoughts whilst on the river. It is a valuable source of information when filling in the fishing diary. Being ever to hand, in the breast pocket of your jacket, it means that accurate totals are kept. These bank notes are valuable, a shortage of a particular fly, the need for a different rod, stronger line, or to remove an awkward branch can all be noted.

There are few things more frustrating than dropping in on a great rise on a brook you have been waiting to fish, only to find the rod you brought keeps getting caught in the summer vegetation and a shorter rod is what you need.

At the end of the day each page can be removed and used as a base for filling in the diary in the evening.

More philosophically, it may record how the setting sun turned a trout red, or the sight of a kingfisher, or how the daffodils looked on the first day of the season.

On Accessories

The basic items above should see the angler through a normal day on the water. They are all lightweight and can be contained in the pockets of your jacket.

Each angler will choose what is important to them, some will reject an item and include another. There are several things that one may see as optional and others as essential, these are considered later.

Think carefully before adding too much to the list however, the Teme and its tributaries are difficult waters to fish. It is not only catching fish that is difficult but also accessing steep banks, nettle beds, briars, long walks and heavily overgrown stretches. These all make fishing a struggle on a hot day: the last thing an angler needs is a heavy bag and a load of tackle. Make it a day to enjoy, not to endure. Less is more, even a pocketful of change can be an irritation when walking all day, and why carry a rod bag when the rods are made up, leave it all in the car. With all you need in the pockets of your jacket, you are freed to enjoy your day. Simplicity is the ultimate sophistication.

So, what of those 'extras', those things that help when fishing in certain situations. Firstly, a landing net. The accounts of days on the river show that it is possible to grasp trout by the point of the lower jaw and hold them, without removing them from the river, to remove the fly. It is a quick and simple operation and should not damage any fish.

However for large trout, grayling and coarse fish you will need a landing net of some sort. On a small stream nets are a nuisance, they catch every trailing bramble and always seem to be left behind as you fish. If you need one, a small net the size and shape of a tennis racket is handy and will engulf all grayling and all but the biggest trout and it can be tucked under your wader belt to hang down your back where it will be to hand and out of the way of briars.

Insect repellent will be needed for those hot summer days when the fly-fisher has to deal with the wrong sort of fly. These pests will attack when all else is going awry and add immeasurably to his frustration. Each will have their own favourite to keep midges, mosquitos or horse flies away. After use wash and wipe your hands or the smell may deter fish and the ingredients may damage fly lines. A cream to soothe the bites and stings that are bound to come your way may be found useful. If the current is strong or the water unfamiliar, a wading staff is useful. Its main use should be to test the water in front to check for steps or drop offs and as a third leg to increase stability. Do not wade on an unfamiliar section if you cannot see the bottom; the Teme can be dangerous. A wading staff is useful for crossing the river and provides security and stability even in shallow water to avoid a stumble, and a dunking.

If you are concerned for your stability and safety, an automatic life jacket is a neat lightweight solution and could save your life. A mobile phone could be added to the list of safety items, and is handy if locked out of the car or for other transport problems.

Some anglers, with a habit of falling in, have a bag of old clothes in the car for when they 'become one with the river', or get soaked in a storm.

A camera is nice to have along to record any exceptional catch. Ensure it is tethered to avoid it slipping into the water; look after it to avoid looking for it.

If you choose to go after late season grayling with bait, different tackle is needed. Rod, reel and line will be exchanged for the appropriate equipment, and jacket pockets can be emptied of fly-fishing tackle, (note pad, first aid kit etc may stay). End tackle in the form of floats, weights and hooks are best carried in a box, which entails a small bag or creel.

A small, square wicker creel will hold a tackle box, bait, food and flask, serve as a seat and yet is lightweight. A square creel however is an awkward thing to carry far, a small backpack or curved shoulder creel is more comfortable and useful if you intend walking far or wading. For more static angling, a combined seat/backpack is ideal.

If you use a landing net for larger coarse fish, grayling or trout, then the choice is between a fixed long handle for bank fishing or a short 'trout net'. A short handle is handy when wading to trot the stream for grayling. A net will also hold your fish in order to weigh it.

On Accessories

A rod rest is handy, though you may hold your rod, there are times when you wish to rest the rod to change tackle, drink coffee (always sure to trigger a bite), or simply rest your arm.

One small aid that may be found useful when wading is the use of a small decorator's paint pot as a bait bucket. These small plastic buckets come with a snap fit lid and wire handle and are ideal to clip to a creel strap or wading belt. They sit upright, open and available when wading and are perfect to hold bait ready for the hook or to be loose-fed into the stream.

A spring balance can be hooked through the mesh of a landing net. Remember, 'A false balance is an abomination to the Lord: but a just weigh is His delight.'.[6]

While fly fishing benefits from minimal tackle requirements, bait fishing on our small border rivers is also a more mobile sport and the ability to move easily along the river bank is a blessing.

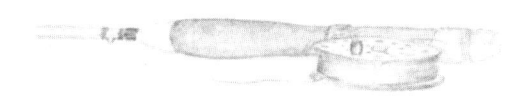

---

[6] Proverbs Chapter II Verse I

TACTICS OF THE MINOR STREAM

Tactics are the way an angler uses tackle, clever ploys used on the river bank. A wider definition includes anything an angler does to improve his fishing. Here are some particular tactics to match the special nature of these Welsh borderland streams.

Firstly, how do these border streams differ from other English rivers and streams? What makes them so special and why are these particular tactics so important?

The border streams are unlike the classic chalkstreams that fill the pages of old fishing books. Neither are they freestone rivers of the northern type with fast flowing gravelly runs and wide-open banks. The limestone rivers of the Peak District and Derbyshire may be similar, but they are not the same.

Border streams need to be considered as a breed apart. An angler will bring skills learnt on other waters to aid him on border streams. He will know not to treat all waters the same and to take into

Tactics of the Minor Stream

account local knowledge. On our border streams he will find a wide variety of waters with features that will influence everything from access, to casting, to tackle and especially tactics.

Methods may be similar to a chalk-stream, upstream dry fly to a rising fish for example; however, on a small overgrown stream the tackle will be adjusted to suit, the cast becomes a sideways 'flick', the stance balanced between nettle beds, tucked under alders or wading midstream. Rarely will the angler see the trout in the water. This is where tactics differ and become important.

Anglers setting out to fish a chalk-stream will check tackle and methods, if only to avoid infringing the rules. Yet the chalk-stream fisherman need not be too concerned about floods or coloured water, the flow and depth are regular, the banks level and even and the access is easy.

The Teme, in contrast, is ever changing. It tumbles from fast run to shallow ford to deep pool at every twist and turn on its ever-winding way down the valley. Fed by the rain falling on Welsh and Shropshire hills the Teme and its tributaries rise and fall like a yo-yo. In spring the border angler waits for the floods to ebb and in high summer the water trickles between sun baked stones. Seasonal variations are magnified on these small waters, such is their changeable nature.

Planning and preparation can produce a good day or at least prevent a disaster. Floods and brief summer spates are a natural hazard on the Teme. They can come at any time, most of the water comes from rain recently fallen in the catchment. Some water is held back in bogs on border hills that act as sponges, however forestry clearance and developments can increase runoff into streams and add to flooding.

Winter is normally the season when the water rises and fishing becomes impractical. High, coloured water and cold temperatures kill the prospect of sport and this often carries over into spring. In a wet spring every little ditch, drain and rivulet will add its load of muddy water to the stream and in no time the river will be, 'running as red as a fox'.

It pays to check water levels. In recent years two of the most destructive floods came in June and

July. Technology has made checking a lot easier. The Environment Agency has monitoring stations at Tenbury, Ludlow, Leintwardine and Knighton on the main river and on the Corve, Onny, Ledwyche and Rea. Levels are shown on their website, so you can check water levels the night before. With that information, and a note in the fishing diary recording previous fishable levels, you may save many wasted journeys.

The upper reaches of the river are usually the first to clear, similarly the streams clear before the main river. The Teme above Knighton runs over gravel and is often clear when lower down it is too coloured to fish. Look at the Lugg and Arrow too, they run over gravels and are less prone to colour than the Teme. You may wish to plan your visit accordingly.

If you choose to fish in coloured water remember first and foremost it can be hazardous. Never wade where you cannot see the bottom on account of the many drops and steps in the river bed. It would be very easy to step into six feet of water and, if it is in flood, it would be difficult to get out again.

Very low water gives the opportunity to study the bottom of the river. Deep holes and gullies that are normally hidden can be noted. When the levels return to normal the angler will have an advantage, especially when choosing a spot for grayling.

To the changes in water must be added the differences in the many and various brooks, streams and small rivers all packed into this small region. All are subtly different in character. They differ in how they react to conditions, one may flood, another clear quickly, one may offer autumn grayling fishing and another the chance of chub or dace. The fly-fisher may look forward to hawthorn fly time on the wooded Ledwyche or the evening rise on the Rea. Hatches of particular flies are worth noting. Arriving on the river just as the action gets under way can lead to a 'red letter day'. If the angler is an 'all round' angler, and I hope he is, he will take any opportunity to observe the fish in the river and thus add to his prospects. Success often comes from detail. Successful anglers take care over what they do. A little research and reconnaissance can increase the likelihood of a fish even before the first cast. He may be fishing for a grayling, but there, tucked in alongside a rocky ledge deep in the run, is a large barbel, mark it for another day. Trout may be the target on a swift ford, but a silver grayling promises the chance of a shoal there in autumn. One evening, whilst barbel fishing, the river came alive with an evening rise, large trout taking struggling spent mayfly into the twilight. Like the trout, the border angler is an opportunist, aware of his surroundings. Serendipity, or just developing the art of seeing, means the angler takes his chances when he can.

Take advantage of being on the river after trout when the coarse fish are spawning. They sometimes can be seen on the gravels and in weed in the early summer. They are not always easy to see but, if you do, it may surprise you to see their numbers and to such a size.

Now having talked about the various waters, the practical angler will want to find out how to access them. Where to find fishing is the first thing the newcomer needs to sort out. Luckily, throughout the Teme valley and the surrounding area fishing is accessible and inexpensive. Anglers living by the chalk-streams of Hampshire may seem fortunate, however for them to find cheap and accessible fishing is far harder than here on the Welsh borders.

For those new to the area, or who can only get to the water occasionally, day tickets are available from tackle shops and some caravan sites. The River Trusts also sell day tickets (voucher scheme), as yet there are few such vouchers for the Teme catchment, but they are a good way to explore different waters.

Once settled on fishing one area, joining a club or association will work out cheaper if you spend much time on the river. As this book was originally to promote the Tenbury Fishing Association, it has to be my first recommendation. With a wealth of fishing over a diverse selection of waters, it remains one of the least expensive. It is usually more productive to learn one section of river than to chase from one place to the next. So choose a club or association that suits you best and learn its waters and take the opportunity to talk to fellow anglers.

For those seriously without cash, and it can happen to anyone, there is free fishing to be had. Public or urban fishing is not for everyone. Waters can be hard fished with spinners and worms, you may compete with dogs retrieving sticks and kids paddling, you may be casting between shopping trolleys and road cones. Think of it as habitat enhancement for trout. Nevertheless it is fishing and, if it is all you can have, make the most of it.

Most of the border towns have a little 'town water'. I will leave you to find your local water, but to get you started, Ludlow, Leominster and Tenbury all have good stretches containing trout and grayling, some surprisingly large.

Asking farmers and landowners directly sometimes works. Much of the land bordering the Teme and its tributaries is let to tenant farmers. The farmer may be able to give permission, usually the landowner retains the sporting rights. Some landowners place sporting rights in the hands of a land agent whose job it is to protect a valuable asset and make money from it.

Farmers can be reticent; they work hard for small return and are not keen to give anything away. They care little about fishing (waste of time) and do not welcome strangers on their land. They are wary of any who come knocking at the door, especially if you have a flashy car and talk funny. Dress smart, smile and be polite. You may get permission for the odd evening. Don't turn up with your mates, take great care of gates and fences (never climb fences), park your car where he knows that it's you fishing and always have something to offer him in return. You need to show that you are not more trouble than you are worth. If the fishing is good, and you are invited back, you may be able to arrange something more permanent. To start, finding the right stream for you may take a little time. A stream of your own may be a distant dream to those living in London or Hampshire, but it is feasible in the Welsh borders. Check the Ordnance Survey map of your area, there are a few small streams that never get fished. On some other waters the angler may have lost interest or become elderly and not fished for years, ask around. Some anglers may be looking for another to share a water with, or you may simply get an invitation as a guest. Having your own fishery is not for everybody, but there are many small streams to be explored.

It is easier to begin on your own. Farmers and landowners like to know who they are dealing with and prefer to talk face to face. Groups and syndicates may get turned down whereas an individual may get in.

What to pay? The least you may reasonably expect. However, remember the cost of alternative fishing. Ask him what he drinks, it is an accepted way of saying you expect to pay something. A 'drink' may be a bottle of whisky or a sum of money, cash of course; it is a gentlemen's agreement and no business of anyone else. It is possible to rent a small stretch of river or stream for a year for less than the cost of having guided fishing on a chalk-stream for a day.

Consider the benefits of your own water. You would never have anyone fishing your favourite spot and, even on a bank holiday, it is not going to be crowded. It also means that you get to make the rules, or not. Best of all it means that you get to know a section of water intimately, to control and create a fishery and in doing so improve it.

Fishing methods are less regulated on border rivers than on chalk-streams or still-waters, How you fish is decided by the quarry and the season rather than the rule book. The ethical angler does more than is required and less than is allowed.

On Tenbury Fishing Association waters trout fishing is with the fly, but wet or dry, upstream or down, one fly or many, the choice is yours. The angler is free to use which method he thinks most suitable[7]. The traditions of wet-fly and dry fly are practised equally and complimentary.

Grayling are splendid sport on the fly but, when autumn comes and cold weather drives them deep, a bait trotted under a float continues the sport. Other coarse fish can be sought with bait in their season.

This ideal arrangement works because the members are anglers, sportsmen who realise fishing should be fun and no one way of fishing is right or wrong so long as it is fair, sporting and within the fishery rules. Some would ban anything

---

[7] "the judicious and perfect application of dry, wet and mid-water fly fishing stamps the finished fly fisher with the hallmark of efficiency" Francis Francis 1867.

they themselves dislike. You should no more tell a man how to fish than you would tell him how to eat his dinner.

By all means help the novice by suggesting an easier or better way, but don't try to impose unfair or prejudiced limitations on another's sport. There are too many unjust rules in life, fishing is an escape from that.

When you fish will influence how you fish; as an angler your tactics change with the seasons. The natural cycle of the seasons govern the waters and the fish follow their rhythm. At the start of the trout fishing season with cold water and little fly life, fishing a wet-fly downstream can be used to search for a taking fish when none are rising. Other anglers may use a heavy nymph to take fish. One time a novice, a guest on a chill spring day on the Rea, caught a good brace when nothing was rising. He tied on a big bushy fly and simply fished it in all the likely places, so that can work too. It doesn't do to be too prescriptive. Each angler will fish in the manner he enjoys.

Once the weather is warm enough for a few flies to hatch, trout will rise in the tributary streams. Early in the season, if a mid-morning start is made, a hatch can be expected around lunchtime. Normally it is the spring olives that start off the party. On small streams the novice can be confident that in early spring the only rises will be trout; indeed, with few exceptions, trout will be the only inhabitants of the smaller tributaries. What is more, on the smaller streams early in the season, casting will be easier before the vegetation has grown up.

Spring comes in waves, with a few warm days, then recedes as winter takes back control. On the Teme, trout are less willing to rise at the start of the season, preferring to feed on the bottom until the mayfly feast has them looking upward. Some days the trout may be few and some days they may be small but, because they are few and small, we will be thankful for them.

For sport at the beginning of the season try fishing the wet-fly. Unless there are fish rising, it is rarely worthwhile flogging away at the river with a dry-fly. As a novice may find it frustrating to fish with little reward, adapt tactics and fish downstream with a wet-fly. There are trout to be found in the sun-warmed shallows of the Teme's fords.

Tactics and methods may change through the day, sometimes by the hour. If the weak spring sunshine warms the water enough for a hatch at lunchtime and a few trout rise to the spring olives, swap to a dry-fly, or maybe fish a soft-hackled fly in the surface film. It pays to be flexible with presentation and adapt to the behaviour of the fish. April is full of hope that May, hopefully fulfils.

When warmer weather arrives and temperatures rise, so do the trout. The angler smells the warm earth, the may-blossom and the wild garlic in the coppice. Everything is growing and on the move. His senses will tell him it is time to get to the river. Along the lanes hawthorn and cow parsley cover verges and hedgerows with white lace. For the first time since winter the angler feels the warmth of his old friend the sun on his back.

The seasons pass and the flies hatch in their appointed order. Trout will dimple the surface of the streams now; it is the time for the dry-fly. On chalk-streams the angler can stalk his fish; on border streams the rising fish tells the angler the two things he needs to know, where the fish is and that he is feeding. Now he knows where and how to present his fly. Angling after all comes down to putting the right fly (or bait) in the right place at the right time. The right fly, in late spring, is usually something small and dark to match the arrival of the hawthorn fly and the black gnat.

The mayfly season sees the trout in all waters making the best of the banquet. It is the prime time to fish the Teme with a dry-fly and, on any water, a mayfly dun or spinner may provoke a monster to rise. The angler too, should make the most of this annual festival starting in mid-May. Some fishermen, with important business to attend to, leave the hatch unfished for several days… such time cannot be regained.

Summer follows hot on the heels of spring. Tactics change again, gone are the huge mayflies and in their place are the fine lines and delicate spinners of the evening rise.

Now the fishing is technical and precise. Slowing down and noticing the surroundings is a tactic that will help focus on details. It may lead to an extra fish; it will enrich your day. The wise man marvels at the commonplace.

Unlike games, angling does not rely on speed or strength. It requires thought and interpretation. Aim to be aware, the river is a classroom without walls, use your senses to notice and observe. How often do we hear, rather than see a rise? When the angler is tuned into the river he will, like the trout, respond to triggers, the touch of a fish amongst the pull of the current or the blink of a rise out of the corner of an eye. He reads the river; its nuances are signposts that point out where the fish may lie.

In summer big catches can be recorded but don't pound the water all day long, wait until after tea and then go down to the river in the cool of the evening and fish on into darkness.

The close and intimate nature of fishing on small border streams leads to a deeper understanding of their hidden details. It is a particular condition of angling on these waters that allows close study of their inhabitants. The mayfly that floats down the stream pulling itself from its shuck, the spinner trapped in the surface film, all happen under the nose of the wading angler. The twists and threads of weaving currents, the flow bringing food over the trout's lie, all are immediate, covered by a sweep of the rod. The small-stream angler has chance to study the minutiae of the stream.

Any guide can only suggest, put forward an opinion. For effective angling the fisher should be able to present a fly both wet and dry, match dun and spinner in order to suit conditions. To fish in the way he enjoys most is the key to pleasure.

Standing in the river, feeling its flow surge around him, the angler is immersed in the river. The push of the current, the swirl and pull as it eddies around him, he is absorbed. He feels the energy of the flow run around him and through him. Then, as he dances the fly down the stream to tempt the trout he is connected to his environment, temporarily transported from one element into another.

If these small streams invite this close connection, then a prudent choice is to avoid anything that gets in the way. The strategy of 'less is more' is one the newcomer should follow. Tackle should be kept to a minimum. On small streams and rivers, presentation is precise. Short, careful casts work best. It is angling in small scale, matching the land of the Teme valley with its little lanes and small fields. This lumpy corner of Shropshire has a charm that the angler will enjoy all the more if he adopts the tactic of minimalist angling and doesn't weigh himself down.

Much clutter can be left in the car. Lunch and flask can be left at a convenient point along the stream rather than lugged up and down banks. Few border streams have open and clear banks; access is often difficult and nothing spoils the day like dragging along unwanted bulk and weight.

A roving approach works well on these small rivers. The tactic is to seek out the fish, try for them while there is any likelihood of sport, before moving on.

Unless you have marked a certain fish or shoal that you want to target, the best chance of finding fish is to try each likely corner in turn. Luckily the Teme is lightly fished and miles can be covered without meeting another angler. The roving angler always has the possibility of meeting an exceptional fish or discovering new productive swims.

By Onny, Teme and Clun

There was a story that American forces in Vietnam were concerned that, while they could destroy the enemy at long range with their superior fire power, if they were forced to fight at close quarters they always came off worse. They tried sending out lightly armed groups to live rough and move constantly to locate the enemy; these groups became ruthlessly effective.

Where this fits into the gentle art of fly-fishing I'm not sure, but it does illustrate an over reliance on equipment can be counterproductive. If you read Hugh Falkus on sea-trout fishing, and you really should, you will see how he treated a fishing trip as a mission with an objective. He was a 'hunter' and a very successful one.

Try to replace tackle with technique. Once you have learnt how to achieve then learn to achieve with less; it is an old philosophy. Perhaps this is taking our gentle pastime a little too seriously, but if you sit exhausted in the hot sun surrounded by all the essentials you think you need, it is something to consider.

The little rivers with their fine fishing have a subtle charm. The streams of the Teme valley are filled with wild trout. They are a most beautiful fish living in the most beautiful surroundings. The streams are difficult, the fishing challenging but not impossible. A good catch from the river is a cause for some satisfaction.

The secret is to enjoy what you have. Any newcomer expecting two-pound trout and ten-pound barbel may well be disappointed; a few exist but they are rarely caught. However, happiness is not measured by the pound. If you can see the beauty in a trout, be it six inches or six pounds, then you can have a good day, whatever the catch. Success as an angler could be the ability to catch whatever is there, regardless of the size, and still have fun.

A true angler will fish for anything; there is no fish, big or small, that he doesn't want to catch. Gudgeon can be fine sport, minnow fishing in search of a perch bait can become a hilarious game. Angling makes us happy. A bobbing float and a silver roach, although only a sprat, makes us smile, just as it did as a boy. On the riverbank the boy returns, adult troubles are carried away by the current, only the boy and the fish are left.

Be practical, large fish are rare. If the maximum size of a trout in a certain stream is twelve inches, be happy with that. Such fish will challenge your angling skills. Use tackle appropriate to the size of the fish. Arthur Ransome described it as 'fishing in Lilliput', small streams, small trout, small tackle. Angling is not a strength test; border streams will test your skill and technique.

Reset your expectations, don't be swayed by targets and pictures of big fish in the media. No one expects to be a champion overnight in simple games like golf or tennis, so why expect it with something as complex as angling? Of course, angling is not a competition, that is what you are escaping from.

Newcomers can find border streams frustrating, they can be physically demanding and challenging to fish, some give up. Adapt to the river, be flexible, forget the text book and be prepared to try some new ways, keep it simple. The wild river is different from the stocked lake. Be persistent: to miss out would be a pity.

The novice looking for the latest tackle set-up or secret rig may be disappointed. Much of what he must learn is practical knowledge that he will gain by spending time by the waterside. A book, even this one, can only point you in the right direction. To seek instructions for every situation is to miss the point, the idea is not to be rigid, bound by instructions, use whatever suits.

With experience you will begin to challenge accepted 'facts', find out what works for you, what you enjoy best. Keep an open mind and explore different methods. The more often you can get to the waterside, the greater the opportunity to gain knowledge. You will get to practice and hone your skills and that leads to greater success.

Casting more often will improve your aim. Casts will be adapted to fit the overgrown stream. Your hand has memory too and, somewhere along the way, casting starts becoming second nature. What a delight when you find your hand better than you thought, the rod becomes an extension of your arm. You begin to enjoy, you no longer have to think and concentrate, frustration turns into satisfaction. Make a habit of success. Habits are very powerful, expect to succeed and you will. Success leads to greater confidence and confidence builds on success.

How then to start? How can you be more successful without catching any more fish? Start easy and start small. Aim to catch a fish, any fish. Then aim to catch one every time you go to the river. It may not happen every time, but carry on. Then try to catch your objective, a trout or a grayling, each time. Then aim for a brace. Sometimes you may fail, we all do: sometimes you may have a bonanza.

Be pleased with your catch each time, even if you haven't caught a fish you will have learnt, become more experienced. A brace of trout, no matter what size, is a triumph. If you are only happy with a two-pound trout, you are not going to be happy very often. Your angling will be happier and richer for thinking small.

More time on the river means a better chance of you being by the water when something good happens. It may be a great hatch of mayfly or a fall of spinners on a perfectly still evening when every trout in the river seemed to rise. These are the times when fishermen say 'You should have been here yesterday'. When you spend a lot of time by the river, the chances are you were.

A FINAL CAST

We have journeyed through the angler's year by various streams. The chill opening day, the mayfly, the evening rise and the grayling: each has its season. Much like the river we have wandered through this little world, this corner of southern Shropshire, along quiet ways with twists and turns and variety enough to fit the angler's moods. It is to be hoped that there has been sufficient of the landscape to please the lover of the countryside and enough trout and grayling to satisfy the angler.

Now this book, this journey into the angling delights of the Marches, must be concluded; it is time to put into context some of the ideas expressed lest, like the river, it rolls on endlessly. As the angling day starts by gathering and checking tackle, the natural order of this book may have been to start with tackle and tactics. However, anglers are always keen to get to the waterside and, for that reason, the section covering days by the river came first.

A Final Cast

Now as there are strands to be picked out and stitched together, ragged threads and themes woven into one and united into some final thoughts, we shall start by reviewing tackle.

In the tackle section the central theme was to travel light. Everything needed to enjoy a day on a rough border stream was discussed from reel to hook. For small streams tackle should be practical, useful and minimal. A selection was suggested to assist the novice and those new to these waters. Personal preference will influence your choice, but even the experienced angler may find some ideas of interest. Anglers are apt to become ensnared by tackle. Travel light, less is more, the less you burden yourself with the more you will enjoy your day.

Border flies were also discussed. A few personal choices were included for anyone wishing to try a new pattern designed for these rough border waters. Flies of the Welsh Marches have long been dressed in particular styles but the need for a simple, general pattern, able to survive rough water and rough casting, is probably the thought to take away from this section.

Tactics came next, a large and diverse subject. Border fishing requires that you find the fishing, find the fish, avoid floods and use effective methods. All of these were covered along with the need to set expectations to match the water being fished. Slow down and appreciate each fish in the context of where it is caught. This is the key point, enjoy each fish. Build on experience by fishing as often as possible and enjoy each of the rivers and streams in turn. Not everything is instant or obvious but these borders waters offer some of the best wild trout fishing in the country.

Part One provided a selection of angling days. Here the aim was to illustrate a typical day on various border streams and to give a realistic idea of what to expect. The important word here is realistic. Too often expectations raised by the angling media set the novice targets he cannot reach: rather he should enjoy each fish that comes along. That is one reoccurring thread. Another is enjoying the complete experience of being at the waterside. Appreciate the sights, the sounds, the smells and even the feel of the river as it pushes against your waders. Take time to notice the first bank martins returning in the spring, the heron, the kingfisher, the smell of the wild garlic in the woods; these things too bring pleasure. The manner improves the matter.

Angling is important. A wide and sweeping statement perhaps, but consider the facts. Angling is as important to the river as the river is to anglers. Anglers protect and preserve the fish in rivers, they monitor water quality by recording insects and invertebrate numbers in the water. These regular checks taken by anglers over the whole catchment are collated and recorded. Such work is as important to the kingfisher and dipper as the trout. Clean water and healthy rivers are the priorities of the angler. He is a trustee, a guardian, few others care so much and spend so much time, effort and cash in preserving the riparian environment. This protection has existed quietly for generations. The Tenbury Fishing Association dates back to 1843 and was founded to protect the river. To stop angling would lay the rivers open to ruin.

Angling is important economically, less obviously than it once was when anglers travelled to the Teme and stayed for the week at local hotels. Now many anglers who come to the area stay in cottages and caravans along the Teme valley. They benefit the local shops and pubs and some return for family holidays or buy property in the area. Anglers and angling groups pay substantial amounts to farmers and landowners for the right to fish their waters. At a time when farming incomes are squeezed, it helps maintain the local infrastructure. Very large amounts of money have been spent on protecting and improving the riparian environment of the Teme and its tributaries. These waters are important on an international scale, the initiatives have been largely funded by the European Community and led by anglers. The money filters down to a local level and to the landowners, farmers, contractors and suppliers involved.

Angling is important to anglers. An obvious statement perhaps, but consider modern life where stress kills; time spent by the river might save your life. There are proven health benefits from spending time by running water and in the vicinity of trees. Time by the river helps smooth out the stress of everyday life; it replaces the competitive with the contemplative. On the river bank you can achieve success without the threat of being judged. No one marks a score card and no one is a loser when it comes to angling, even a blank day is enjoyable. When we start, we all want to catch fish, many fish, all the time. As we spend more time by the water, we understand that constant catching is not only impossible, but also undesirable. Nothing would quench the excitement quicker than the certain knowledge you were going to catch fish.

Finally, angling is important, but it need not be serious. Sometimes it is simply enough to go angling. Perhaps this is less of a 'how to' book and more of a 'why we do'. It may spur the novice and inspire those discouraged by the trend for instant fishing with results at all costs.

This book has often flooded, over topped its boundaries, and flowed into strange new fields; angling is hard to confine and reduce to neat rules. In angling there are few simple solutions or easy answers to assure a good result every time. Anyone who says they have the secret to consistent catches only fool themselves but we need not be concerned, a day by the river will still be enjoyable.

Having reached thus far you will realise there are no secrets revealed as to how to capture monsters, no fly guaranteed to provoke a rise every time. Sorry, did you expect there to be?

Throughout, the beautiful Welsh border country has been the backdrop to our excursion. Surrounded by all the wonders of the natural world, the angler develops a high regard for nature. True anglers see the value of each fish they catch, they have respect for them, large or small. More anglers are coming to realise that good fishing for true wild trout has great value that once lost, stocking cannot replace. In the same way one could knock down Ludlow Castle and re-build it, but it wouldn't be the same.

For a creature that cannot see the landscape that surrounds it, trout choose to live in some of the most beautiful places. Beautiful landscape should truly be counted part of a nation's wealth and here in the valley of the Teme we enjoy riches. It is almost as if there were two Englands, the modern

A Final Cast

urban and the rural. This is old England, small fields, small farms, small rivers and soft hills; such places are still to be found, if you know where to look.

There is something about fly-fishing that is particularly suited to the British countryside; it is a winding country lane not a motorway. It is the angler's skill to appreciate small things, details, to observe and understand and for those who do there are wonders.

The angler whose jewels are the kingfisher and the trout is rich. His priceless landscapes are not painted and hung on a wall, but surround him. He sees the miraculous in the mundane, such marvels are rarely to be found in city streets.

Whereas not every fishing trips ends with a haul of fish, each time will take you to some special places. This is the English countryside at its best where the little rivers of the Welsh Marches flow past history-haunted places. Small streams well loved by anglers and often small trout too, but the rewards are great. Returning home from the river on one of those wonderful days when it is difficult not to feel sorry for those who have the misfortune to be anywhere else in the world; then at the end of such a day, when the angler is lifted higher than the angels, he might think, 'You may have the world, if I may have south Shropshire.' My word! Forgive me, my friend, I fear I am getting too much fire in the blood. Yet it is hard not to sing the praises for a land and a sport for which one feels such a passion.

These are the ties that bind the angler by the finest of lines that stretch no matter how far he roams, and at a touch can turn his head for home, bound by the strongest of bonds. The Japanese believe that ghosts appear where willow trees grow by the water. Could it be that finding no better haven than this earthly paradise, they are reluctant to move on?

Despite the wonderful improvements to tackle and the countless words and images dedicated to their capture, the fish remain the same. A trout is still a trout, the same trout that I fished for as a boy, the fish do not change nor do the rivers in which they swim. There stands a castle at Ludlow, those stones were laid by Norman hands, the same

A Final Cast

hands may have fished the river with the same hopes as we do now. A thousand years are as nothing, the fish remain, the river remains, the trout still rise to the same fly.

Alas, dear reader, it is getting late. The ash is gathering in the grate and the flames are nearly out. Time to reel in for the last time, for in the twilight at the end of the day, the last cast is the hardest. Like an addict we always want one more. It is difficult to finish the fishing day. There is always the thought that the next cast will land the fly in front of a fish of a lifetime. It may be that the best time to end the day is late evening when gathering darkness draws the day inexorably to a close and the fly is lost from sight.

I hope you have enjoyed reading this as much as I have enjoyed writing it, and if you went down to the river, or caught just one more fish as a result, then smile, my friend, and whisper my name, for I may be one of those who still haunt the river's banks.

~*~

FINIS